THE WAY WE USED TO Cook

A note on ingredients

Some ingredients in this book are given in spoon and cup measurements while others, for precision, are given in ounces and grams. Note that 1 teaspoon = 5g = ¼oz = 5ml, 1 tablespoon = 15g = ½oz = 15ml. Liquid measures: 1 cup = 9fl oz (250ml). Solid measures vary depending on the ingredient. For the following key ingredients, conversions are approximately as follows: 1 cup superfine (caster) sugar = 7oz (220g); 1 cup flour = 5oz (150g); 1 cup confectioner's (icing) sugar = 5oz (150g); 1 cup raisins = 5½oz (170g).

First published in 2013 by
New Holland Publishers
London • Sydney • Cape Town • Auckland
www.newhollandpublishers.com

Garfield House 86–88 Edgware Road London W2 2EA United Kingdom
1/66 Gibbes Street Chatswood NSW 2067 Australia
Wembley Square First Floor Solan Road Gardens Cape Town 8001 South Africa
218 Lake Road Northcote Auckland New Zealand

Managing director: Fiona Schultz
Publisher: Fiona Schultz
Project editor: Kate Sherington
Designer: Lorena Susak
Production director: Olga Dementiev
Printer: Toppan Leefung Printing Limited

Follow New Holland Publishers on
Facebook: www.facebook.com/NewHollandPublishers

THE WAY WE USED TO

Cook

TRADITIONAL RECIPES FOR DELICIOUS
HOME COOKING

JUNE HOLM

NEW
HOLLAND

.CONTENTS.

SCRUMPTIOUS SOUPS AND SALADS

...

SCRUMPTIOUS SOUPS
AND SALADS

ɵɵɵ

Nothing is more warming in winter than gorgeous, freshly-made soup, or more refreshing in summer than a light, crisp salad.

Whatever the season, this chapter will equip you with truly classic recipes in both domains. These meals will all make excellent small suppers, starters or sides, as well as satisfying lunches.

ɵ ADVICE FOR SOUP ɵ

Although fresh ingredients and stock will often taste better, purchased stock and frozen vegetables can work just as well. You can also dice fresh vegetables, then freeze them in plastic bags, ready for later use. Canned diced tomatoes are always helpful to have on hand.

Many soups require some starch for thickening, in the form of rice, noodles or barley. You don't need much, as the amount added will tend to increase in volume as it absorbs liquid.

Wine can be an excellent addition, which should be added at a ratio of no more than ¼ cup per quart (litre) of soup. If you wish to add cream or milk, stir it through when the soup is off the boil, to prevent curdling – then you can bring the soup back to a simmer before serving. The taste of herbs will be more intense if they are added late in the cooking process. Use them with care, as you don't want to overwhelm the vegetables.

ɵ ADVICE FOR SALAD ɵ

Salads are said to be ancient in origin, but more lately came into regular use in the early 20th century, becoming especially popular in the 1960s. This revivial produced such modern classics as potato salad, coleslaw and the ubiquitous Greek and Caesar salads we see at restaurants and backyard barbecues today.

The key in a salad is to keep things simple. Don't drown it in dressing – in fact, to keep everyone happy, you may wish to serve dressing on the side. Think about presentation by using ingredients that complement each other in terms of style and texture, and try to use what is in season for the best-tasting results. Leftover vegetables, grains and protein can be put to good use in salads.

MINESTRONE

⅓ cup olive oil

1 medium brown onion, sliced

1 clove garlic, crushed

9oz (250g) potatoes, peeled and chopped

5oz (150g) carrots, thinly sliced

4oz (125g) celery, thinly sliced

5oz (150g) zucchini (courgette), sliced

4 cups vegetable stock

14oz (400g) canned Roma tomatoes

rind from piece of Parmesan cheese

¼ cup parsley, chopped

14oz (400g) canned cannellini beans

salt and freshly ground black pepper

Serves 6

◦ Heat the oil in a saucepan and cook the onion and garlic for 5 minutes until onion is tender. Add the potatoes and cook for a further 5 minutes. Repeat with the carrots, celery and courgette.

◦ Add the beef stock, tomatoes and cheese rind, bring to the boil and simmer covered for 1 hour. If the soup becomes too thick, add more stock.

◦ Add the chopped parsley and cannellini beans, and heat for a further 10 minutes.

◦ To serve, remove the cheese rind, season with salt and black pepper, and serve with crusty bread.

GOULASH

3 tablespoons olive oil

2 medium white onions,
   sliced

2 tablespoons Hungarian
   (mild) paprika

2 cloves garlic, minced

2 teaspoons caraway seeds

8 sprigs fresh marjoram,
   leaves removed and stalks
   discarded

17½oz (500g) diced beef

14oz (400g) canned diced
   tomatoes

2 tablespoons tomato paste

6 cups beef stock

2 teaspoons brown sugar

1 teaspoon salt

1 teaspoon black pepper

14oz (400g) potatoes, diced

7oz (200g) carrots, diced

1 tablespoon cornstarch
   (cornflour), mixed with
   2 tablespoons cold water

¼ cup sour cream

2 pickled cucumbers, finely
   diced

3 cooked Frankfurters, finely
   sliced (optional)

Serves 8

◦ Heat the olive oil in a saucepan and sauté the onion
until golden brown, about 5 minutes. Add the paprika,
garlic, caraway seeds and marjoram and cook for 1–2
minutes until the mixture is fragrant.

◦ Add the beef, diced tomatoes and tomato paste, and
cook until the meat is well coated and is a rich brown,
about 5 minutes. Add the stock, sugar, salt and pepper
and bring to the boil. Simmer for 1 hour. Add the
potatoes, carrots and continue cooking for a further 30
minutes.

◦ Check seasonings and adjust if necessary. Stir the
cornstarch mixture into the soup, mixing well. Allow
the soup to thicken for a couple of minutes, then serve
in individual bowls.

◦ Garnish with sour cream, cucumbers and Frankfurters,
if using.

OXTAIL SOUP

1 oxtail
1 tablespoon seasoned
  all-purpose (plain) flour
2 tablespoons oil
6 cups beef stock
1 carrot, sliced
1 small turnip, sliced
1 onion, roughly chopped
2 stalks celery, chopped
2–3 bay leaves
salt
pinch of cayenne pepper
juice of 1 lemon
1 teaspoon Worcestershire
  sauce
3 tablespoons sherry or
  Madeira

Serves 8

- Coat oxtail in seasoned flour. Heat oil over a medium heat, add oxtail and cook until brown. Add stock and simmer for 2 hours. Skim off the froth.
- Place vegetables and bay leaves in the stock and cook for a further 15–20 minutes.
- Remove meat from bones, return the meat to soup and reheat. Season with salt and cayenne pepper. Stir in lemon juice and Worcestershire sauce. Just before serving, add sherry.

CABBAGE SOUP

1oz (30g) butter
9oz (250g) beef, diced
4oz (125g) bacon pieces
10½oz (300g) cabbage,
  finely shredded
2 large tomatoes, peeled and
  diced
2 onions, diced
1 bay leaf
salt and freshly ground black
  pepper
4 cups beef stock
⅓ cup sour cream
1½oz (40g) Parmesan
  cheese, grated

Serves 6

- Melt butter in a large saucepan and sauté beef and bacon over a medium heat until browned.
- Add half the cabbage and all the remaining ingredients except sour cream and Parmesan. Cover, bring to the boil, and simmer for 1½ hours.
- Add remaining cabbage and cook for 10–15 minutes or until tender. Stir in cream, sprinkle with Parmesan cheese and serve.

CHICKEN VEGETABLE SOUP

2 skinless chicken breast
  fillets
4 cups chicken stock
1 tablespoon canola oil
2 leeks, washed and thinly
  sliced
2 carrots, diced
2 stalks celery, diced
3 cloves garlic, crushed
6 cups young green leaves
  (watercress, rocket, sorrel,
  baby spinach), washed
3 tablespoons fresh pesto
freshly cracked black pepper

Cheese sticks
1 sheet puff pastry
1½oz (40g) Cheddar
  cheese, finely grated

Serves 6

- Put the chicken in a pot, add just enough chicken stock to cover it and poach gently for about 10 minutes, or until just cooked. Set aside to cool.
- Heat the oil in a large pot, add the leeks and cook gently for about 2 minutes until soft. Add the carrot, celery and garlic, strain the chicken poaching stock through a fine sieve and add to the vegetables with the rest of the stock. Simmer for 10 minutes.
- Chop the greens finely, add them to the soup and cook for a further 10 minutes.
- Tear the chicken breasts into fine shreds and add them to the soup. Stir in the pesto and season with plenty of cracked black pepper.

Cheese sticks
- Preheat the oven to 430°F (220°C). Cut the puff pastry into ¾in (2cm) thick strips and place on a baking tray lined with baking paper. Sprinkle with the cheese and bake for 20 minutes or until crisp and golden.
- Serve the soup in wide bowls with cheese sticks.

OLD-STYLE CHICKEN BROTH

2lb 4oz (1kg) chicken
 pieces, breasts and thighs
1 lemon, sliced
1 teaspoon salt
freshly ground black pepper
1 bay leaf
3 tablespoons medium-grain
 rice
2 carrots, thinly sliced
1 stalk celery, sliced
2 leeks, washed thoroughly
 and sliced, or 2 white
 onions, thinly sliced
¼ cup parsley, chopped

Serves 4

- Where possible, remove skin from chicken. Pour over 8 cups cold water with lemon slices and allow to soak half an hour.
- Bring lemon water to boil. Add salt, pepper and bay leaf, then simmer for 30 minutes.
- Add rice and continue to cook for an extra 40 minutes. When chicken is quite tender, remove from broth.
- Remove any remaining chicken skin. Dice chicken into small pieces. Replace in broth, check seasoning, then cool and skim fat from broth.
- Reheat and serve sprinkled with parsley.

CHICKEN AND LEEK SOUP

2lb 4oz (1kg) boiling
   chicken
1 onion, chopped
1 carrot, peeled and chopped
pinch of saffron
1 stalk celery, chopped
2 leeks, finely sliced
1oz (30g) butter
salt
cayenne pepper
½ cup light whipping
   (thickened) cream

Serves 6

- In a large pot, place the chicken, onion, carrot, saffron and celery. Cover the ingredients with water and boil for 1 hour.
- Remove from the heat and strain off the stock. Reserve the chicken.
- Sauté the leeks in the butter until soft. Add the chicken stock and heat through. Season with salt and cayenne pepper. Add cream as desired and serve.

LAMB SHANK AND VEGETABLE SOUP

4 lamb shanks, French
   trimmed
3 stalks celery, cut into ¼in
   (1cm) pieces
2 medium carrots, peeled
   and cut into ¼in (1cm)
   pieces
1 rutabaga (swede), peeled
   and cut into ¼in (1cm)
   cubes
1 parsnip, peeled and cut
   into ¼in (1cm) cubes
1lb 12oz (800g) canned
   tomato soup
⅓ cup flat-leaf parsley,
   coarsely chopped
salt and freshly ground
   black pepper

Serves 6

- Combine lamb shanks, celery, carrot, rutabaga, parsnip, tomato soup and 6 cups cold water in a large saucepan over high heat and bring to the boil. Reduce heat to low and simmer, covered, stirring occasionally, for 2¼ hours or until the lamb is tender and falling away from the bone.
- Remove from heat and stir in parsley. Use tongs to remove the bones. Taste and season with salt and pepper. Ladle soup into bowls and serve with crusty bread.

CORN AND BACON CREAM SOUP

6 rashers bacon, rind
   removed, chopped
1 medium onion, thinly
   sliced
17½oz (500g) potatoes,
   peeled and medium diced
29½oz (880g) canned
   creamed sweetcorn
3 cups milk
1 sprig thyme, leaves
   removed and stalk
   discarded
salt and freshly ground
   black pepper
dash of Worcestershire sauce

Serves 8

- Place bacon in a saucepan and sautè over medium heat until crisp. Remove and drain on absorbent paper.
- Sautè onion until tender, add potatoes and 5 cups boiling water and cook for a further 10 minutes.
- Add sweetcorn, milk, thyme and bacon, bring to the boil, season with salt, pepper and Worcestershire sauce. Garnish with extra fresh thyme or parsley.

LAMB SOUP

1 tablespoon olive oil
1 large brown onion,
 finely chopped
17½oz (500g) stewing
 lamb, finely chopped
⁷oz (200g) canned
 chickpeas, rinsed and
 drained
3 tablespoons tomato purée
1 teaspoon ground cilantro
 (coriander)
1 teaspoon ground turmeric
½ teaspoon chilli powder
½ teaspoon salt
1½ tablespoons dried mint
juice of ½ lemon
6 fresh mint sprigs
1 lemon, cut into wedges

Serves 6

○ Heat the oil in a large casserole or saucepan. Gently fry the onion for a few minutes until pale golden and soft.
○ Add the lamb, chickpeas, tomato purée, spices and salt, cooking for a few more minutes and stirring well.
○ Add 4 cups water to the saucepan – this should cover the mixture – then add 1 cup more if required. If adding extra water, remember that you may need to add a little extra spice and salt to compensate.
○ Cover and simmer over a medium heat for approximately 45–50 minutes or until the lamb is tender. If required, you may add a little extra water again at this point, but remember to adjust the seasoning if you do.
○ Add the dried mint and the lemon juice, return to the heat for a further 3–4 minutes, then serve each bowl with a sprig of fresh mint and a lemon wedge on the side.

PEA SOUP

9oz (250g) split peas
17½oz (500g) bacon bones
2 carrots, roughly chopped
2 turnips, roughly chopped
2 onions, roughly chopped
4 stalks celery, chopped
salt and freshly ground
   black pepper
1 tablespoon all-purpose
   (plain) flour, mixed with
   1 tablespoon water

Serves 8

- Wash peas and soak in water overnight. Place peas, water and bones in a saucepan and bring to the boil. Add prepared vegetables and simmer for 1½ hours.
- Remove bones, purée mixture, and season with salt and pepper. Thicken with flour paste and, stirring continuously, cook for 3 minutes.
- Garnish with croutons and serve immediately.

CREAM OF CAULIFLOWER SOUP

1lb 10oz (750g) cauliflower florets
7oz (200g) onions, chopped
6 cups chicken stock
6 cups milk
2 teaspoons salt
¼ teaspoon cayenne pepper
½ cup light whipping (thickened) cream
¼ cup parsley, chopped

Serves 8

- Combine the cauliflower, onions, stock and milk in a large boiling pot. Cook until the cauliflower has broken down. Remove from heat.
- Blend the cauliflower and liquid, then return to the pot.
- Season with salt and cayenne pepper, then add the cream. Reheat and serve garnished with chopped parsley.

TOMATO SOUP

1lb 10oz (750g) ripe
  tomatoes, chopped
1 potato, peeled and
  chopped
1 small onion, chopped
1 sprig fresh basil
1 teaspoon sugar
2 tablespoons tomato paste
salt and freshly ground black
  pepper
1 cup vegetable stock
¼ cup light whipping
  (thickened) cream
¼ cup parsley, finely
  chopped

Serves 4

- Place all ingredients, except parsley and cream, into a saucepan with the stock. Bring to the boil and simmer, covered, for 20 minutes.
- Serve soup with a swirl of cream and sprinkle with chopped parsley.

PUMPKIN SOUP

3lb 5oz (1½kg) pumpkin, peeled and cut into large cubes
2 tomatoes, chopped
1 large onion, chopped
5 cups vegetable stock
pinch of salt
pinch of cayenne pepper
⅔ cup light whipping (thickened) cream
¼ cup parsley, finely chopped

Serves 6

- Combine pumpkin, tomato and onions with the stock in a pan. Simmer gently until pumpkin is tender, approximately 20 minutes.
- Purée pumpkin mixture. Return to pan, add salt, cayenne pepper and cream and reheat gently.
- Serve sprinkled with parsley.

CHICKEN NOODLE SOUP

3⅔ cups chicken stock

1 bay leaf

1 onion, halved

8oz (250g) skinless chicken
   breast

2oz (60g) vermicelli noodle,
   broken into smaller pieces

salt and freshly ground black
   pepper, to taste

1 tablespoon fresh parsley,
   chopped, to garnish

Serves 4–6

- Put chicken stock, bay leaf, onion and chicken breast into a large saucepan over a high heat. Cook until the mixture is boiling, stirring once or twice.
- Reduce heat to a simmer and cook for 10 minutes or until chicken is tender.
- Lift chicken out of the saucepan with a draining spoon and cut into very small pieces. Lift out onion and bay leaf and discard. Bring stock back to the boil, add vermicelli and cook for 7 minutes or until *al dente*.
- Return chopped chicken to the pan and season with salt and pepper, then heat through.
- Ladle into warm soup bowls and sprinkle with chopped parsley to serve.

PEA AND HAM SOUP

1lb (500g) dried split peas
2lb (1kg) bacon bones
4 pints (2.5L) chicken stock
2 Frankfurters
2 teaspoons white vinegar
sliced sour gherkins, to
   garnish

Serves 8

- Soak peas overnight. Drain. Add peas and bacon bones to stock, bring to the boil and simmer for 2½ hours.
- Cool soup and remove bacon bones. Scrape meat off bones and return meat to soup. Cook frankfurters in boiling water for 3 minutes. Cool frankfurters, then peel them and cut them into ¼ in (5mm) slices. Add to soup, with white vinegar. Reheat soup and serve with sour gherkins.

WARM HERBED POTATO SALAD

3lb (1⅓kg) russet or Idaho
   potatoes
2 tablespoons olive oil
4 white onions, sliced
¼ cup dill, chopped
¼ cup chervil, chopped
¼ cup Italian parsley,
   chopped
zest of 1 lemon

Dressing
⅔ cup extra-virgin olive oil
⅓ cup white wine vinegar
juice of 1 lemon
3 cloves garlic
salt and freshly ground
   pepper

Serves 6–8

- Cut the unpeeled and well washed potatoes into large chunks, place in a saucepan, and boil in salted water for 10 minutes, or until tender but not soft.
- In a heavy-based skillet, heat the oil and sauté the onions over a high heat until golden, about 8 minutes. Reduce the heat, cover, and cook slowly for 20 minutes to caramelize the onions.
- Drain the potatoes and return to the saucepan.
- In a small bowl, whisk the dressing ingredients until thickened. Pour the dressing over the hot potatoes and toss, adding the fresh herbs and lemon zest with salt and lots of pepper to taste.
- Add the caramelized onions and toss thoroughly.

CLASSIC POTATO SALAD

2lb (1kg) new potatoes
⅓ cup dry white wine
½ cup vinaigrette dressing
½ cup mayonnaise or ¼
  cup each of sour cream and
  mayonnaise
1 red onion, sliced into rings
1 stalk celery, sliced
2 dill pickles or gherkins,
  thinly sliced
1 teaspoon capers
4 hard-boiled eggs, peeled
  and sliced
¼ cup parsley, chopped
salt and freshly ground black
  pepper

Serves 4

- Scrub and boil the potatoes in salted water until tender. Peel and slice them while still hot and place into a bowl. Sprinkle with wine, turning the potato slices carefully.
- Next, sprinkle with the vinaigrette dressing, then stir in mayonnaise. Toss with remaining ingredients. Season with salt and pepper to serve.

GREEK SALAD

2 cucumbers, sliced
4 Roma tomatoes, quartered
2 red onions, quartered
3oz (90g) feta, crumbled
½ cup Kalamata olives, left
  whole
3 tablespoons extra-virgin
  olive oil
2 tablespoons red wine
  vinegar
pinch of sea salt
freshly ground black pepper
¼ cup oregano leaves

Serves 4

◦ Place the cucumber, tomatoes, onion, feta, and olives in a bowl.
◦ Combine olive oil and vinegar in a separate bowl, and whisk. Pour dressing over the salad, then season with salt and pepper.
◦ Garnish with oregano leaves. Serve salad on its own or with fresh bread.

CAESAR SALAD

2 cloves garlic, minced
6 tablespoons extra-virgin
   olive oil
9 anchovies
juice of 1½ lemons
½ teaspoon Worcestershire
   sauce
½ teaspoon mustard
2 tablespoons white wine
   vinegar
4 eggs, boiled for 1 minute
2 thick slices of white bread
salt and freshly ground black
   pepper
4oz (125g) bacon
3 heads of romaine lettuce
2 tablespoons Parmesan,
   shaved

Serves 6

- Preheat the oven to 430°F (220°C).
- In a large mixing bowl, place the minced garlic and 4 tablespoons olive oil and, using the base of a metal spoon, mash the garlic into the oil. Add the anchovies and mash these into the oil mixture as well. Whisk in the lemon juice, Worcestershire sauce, mustard, and white wine vinegar, mixing thoroughly to incorporate each ingredient before the next is added.
- Crack the eggs carefully after they have been boiled for 1 minute, discard the whites, and add the yolks to the mixing bowl. Mix these in thoroughly, incorporating them into the other ingredients. Season to taste with salt. Set aside.
- Cut the bread into cubes and toss with the remaining olive oil and salt and pepper. Transfer to a baking sheet and bake the cubes until golden, about 15 minutes. Leave to cool.
- Crisp the bacon in a frying pan, then break into smaller pieces.
- Place the well-washed lettuce leaves in a mixing bowl and toss them thoroughly in the dressing for several minutes, until all the leaves have been coated. Add the bread cubes and Parmesan and finish with black pepper and crisp bacon. Serve immediately.

WALDORF SALAD WITH CHEDDAR

6oz (170g) red cabbage,
  finely shredded
4 stalks celery, sliced
5oz (150g) Cheddar cheese,
  cut into ½in (12mm)
  cubes
3oz (90g) seedless red
  grapes, halved
2 red apples, cored and
  chopped
1 head of lettuce, leaves torn
½ teaspoon poppy seeds

Dressing
½ cup (150g) plain yogurt
2 tablespoons mayonnaise
1 teaspoon fresh lemon juice
  or white wine vinegar
salt and freshly ground black
  pepper

Serves 4

- To make the dressing, mix together the yogurt, mayonnaise, lemon juice or vinegar, and seasoning.
- In a large bowl, combine the cabbage, celery, Cheddar, grapes and apples, then toss with the dressing.
- Divide the lettuce leaves between plates and top with the cabbage and cheese mixture. Sprinkle with poppy seeds before serving.

MIXED SALAD

1 red capsicum (pepper),
  seeded and cut into
  quarters
3 vine-ripened tomatoes, cut
  into wedges
1 tablespoon olive oil
1 small cucumber, sliced
1 small red onion, finely
  chopped
½ cup black olives
5oz (150g) mixed greens
¼ cup cilantro (coriander)
  leaves

Dressing
¼ cup extra-virgin olive oil
1 tablespoon lemon juice
1 tablespoon red wine
  vinegar
½ teaspoon sugar
salt and freshly ground black
  pepper

Serves 4

- Place capsicum on a baking sheet and broil for
  6–8 minutes, or until skin is blistered and blackened.
  Leave to cool. Remove skin and thinly slice.
- Preheat oven to 360°F (180°C). Place tomatoes on a
  baking sheet lined with parchment paper. Lightly spray
  or brush with olive oil and season with salt and pepper.
  Bake for 15–20 minutes or until just soft. Set aside.
- Combine capsicum, tomatoes, cucumber, red onion,
  olives, salad leaves, and cilantro in a large serving bowl.
- Combine ingredients for dressing in a small bowl. Pour
  dressing over salad and toss to combine.

WINNING DINNERS

...

WINNING DINNERS

∘∘∘

The evening meal can sometimes be our only opportunity, in the course of a busy day, to spend time with our partner, friends or family. That's why it's so important for dinner-time to feature good, fresh meals, made the old-fashioned way – with love.

Cooking from scratch, rather than using pre-packaged meals or sauces, is not nearly as hard as it sounds. It only takes a little more time, and offers a great many more rewards, both in terms of taste and personal satisfaction. It is also a more economical option, particularly if you're good about eating up your leftovers and sticking to a weekly meal plan. Then again, sometimes a little cheating can save the day, so judge as you see fit!

It really helps to be organized – plan the week's menu in advance, and buy what you need in a weekly shop, so that all the ingredients will be at your fingertips. You could even cook some parts of a meal, like pasta sauces, in advance and freeze them for later use.

The old principles of nutrition still hold up. Most of us aim for five portions of fruit and vegetables a day, and many of these will come at dinner-time, especially when we might be skipping breakfast or lunch (tsk, tsk). Consider adding a side of steamed greens to your meal; seasoning spinach with a squeeze of lemon can make all the difference for someone who's squeamish about vegetables. Keep portions of meat to a reasonable size and try to incorporate fish every week. Today, we have learned to eat less red meat than our forebears, but it's still a delicious source of iron and other nutrients, and is perfectly acceptable in moderation.

In this chapter, we have featured all the traditional classics for dinner – delicious pastas, casseroles, pies, oven-bakes and more, sure to please even the picky eaters at your table.

SHEPHERD'S PIE

17½oz (500g) ground
(minced) lamb
1lb 10oz (750g) potatoes,
peeled and cut into chunks
1 teaspoon salt
2 tablespoons vegetable oil
1 medium onion, peeled and
chopped
1 stick celery, diced
1 medium carrot, peeled and
diced
1 tablespoon tomato purée
2 tablespoons Worcestershire
sauce
¾ cup lamb stock
salt and black pepper
¾oz (25g) butter
¼ cup whole milk

Serves 4

- Remove lamb from refrigerator and bring to room temperature. Put the potatoes into a saucepan, cover with cold water and add the salt. Boil for 20 minutes or until tender.
- Meanwhile, preheat the oven to 400°F (200°C). Heat the oil in a large heavy-based frying pan over a medium heat, then fry the onion, celery and carrot for 2–3 minutes, until softened.
- Add the lamb to the pan, breaking it up with a wooden spoon. Cook for 5 minutes or until browned, stirring all the time. Stir in the tomato purée and Worcestershire sauce, mixing well. Cook for 2 minutes. Add the stock, stir, season to taste with salt and black pepper, then simmer for 5 minutes.
- Meanwhile, drain the potatoes and return them to the pan. Add the butter and milk, then mash until smooth.
- Spoon the lamb mixture into a deep ovenproof dish, about 6 x 10in (15 x 25cm) in size. Top with the mashed potatoes, spreading them evenly and fluffing up the surface with a fork. Cook for 20 minutes or until the top is golden brown.

FISH PIE

17½oz (500g) potatoes,
  peeled and cut into even-
  sized pieces
salt and freshly ground
  black pepper
2½oz (75g) butter
2 medium eggs
17½oz (500g) cod fillets
9oz (250g) smoked
  haddock fillets
1½ cups whole milk
⅓ cup all-purpose (plain)
  flour
⅓ cup fresh parsley, finely
chopped

Serves 4

- Put the potatoes into a saucepan, cover with cold water, add ½ teaspoon of salt, then boil for 20 minutes or until tender. Drain and return to the pan. Mash well with a potato masher or fork, then mix in two-thirds of the butter.
- Meanwhile, boil the eggs for 10 minutes in a small pan. Cool under cold running water, then shell and roughly chop. Preheat the oven to 400°F (200°C).
- Place the cod and haddock fillets skin-side down in a frying pan that is large enough to hold them in a single layer. Cover with milk and cook over a medium heat for 10 minutes or until the fish turns opaque.
- Drain the fish, reserving the milk for the sauce, then remove and discard any skin. Using a fork, flake the flesh into thick chunks, removing any bones.
- Place the remaining butter in a large heavy-based saucepan. Melt over a low heat, add the flour and stir to form a smooth paste. Cook for 2 minutes, stirring, to remove the raw taste of the flour. Take off the heat and add the milk little by little, stirring constantly so there are no lumps.
- Put the pan back on the heat and cook the sauce for 5–7 minutes, until quite thick. Take it off the heat again and gently stir in the fish, eggs and parsley. Season well, then pour into a 9 x 6in (23 x 15cm) ovenproof dish. Smooth the mashed potato on top, then fluff it up with a fork. Bake for 30 minutes or until the top turns golden.

CORNED SILVERSIDE WITH WHITE SAUCE

3–4lb (1.5–2kg) piece
  corned silverside or brisket,
  rinsed
1 tablespoon brown sugar
12 whole black peppercorns
1 bay leaf
1 tablespoon vinegar
boiled carrots, onions and
  parsley sprigs, to garnish

White sauce
1oz (30g) butter
1oz (30g) plain flour
1¼ cups milk
salt and freshly ground black
  pepper, to taste

Serves 6–8

- Place silverside in a deep saucepan and cover with cold water. Add remaining ingredients. Bring to simmering point and cook, covered, for 2 hours.
- Garnish with carrots and onions and sprigs of parsley, and serve with white sauce

White sauce

- Melt butter in a saucepan over a low heat, then remove from heat and stir in flour.
- Return to heat and cook gently for a few minutes, making sure that the roux does not brown.
- Remove pan from heat and gradually blend in cold milk.
- Replace pan on heat and bring to the boil. Reduce heat and cook, stirring with a wooden spoon, until smooth.
- Season well. If any lumps have formed, whisk briskly.

- NOTE Corned silverside can also be served cold. Allow to cool in the cooking liquid, and when cold, wrap in plastic clingwrap or aluminium foil and store in the refrigerator.

MEAT PATTY WITH MASHED POTATO

1 egg
¼ cup milk
1½lb (750g) fine ground
  (minced) meat
2oz (60g) breadcrumbs
1 tablespoon red wine
1 carrot, grated
1 zucchini (courgette),
  grated
1 onion, grated
1 teaspoon soy sauce
dash of Worcestershire sauce
⅓ cup all-purpose (plain)
  flour
1 tablespoon butter

Mashed potatoes
4 medium-sized potatoes,
  peeled
½ cup milk
1oz (30g) butter
2oz (60g) tasty cheese,
  grated
salt and freshly ground black
  pepper, to taste

Serves 4

- Beat egg and milk together in a large bowl. Add meat and all other ingredients, except flour and butter, and mix well.
- Spread flour onto a cutting board. Form meat mixture into balls and roll in flour. Then flatten (with a spatula or knife) into patties and place on greaseproof paper. Continue until all mixture has been used.
- Heat butter in a frying pan over a low heat. Place patties in the frying pan and cook for 5 minutes, or until the bottom is golden brown, then turn and continue to cook for 10 minutes, or until golden brown on the other side and cooked through.
- Serve with vegetables and creamy mashed potato.

Mashed potatoes
- Place potatoes into a saucepan with cold, lightly salted water to cover. Bring to the boil and cook gently, covered, for 20–30 minutes, until potatoes are easily pierced with a fork. Drain thoroughly, then shake pan over heat for a minute or two until all surplus moisture has evaporated and potatoes are quite dry.
- Mash potatoes, then beat with a wooden spoon until very smooth.
- In a saucepan, heat milk and butter. Once mixture is hot, add to potatoes and beat until light and fluffy. Add cheese and stir through until melted. Season with salt and pepper.

PORK STEAKS WITH MUSHROOM SAUCE

1 tablespoon vegetable oil
4 pork shoulder steaks,
   trimmed of excess fat
freshly ground black pepper

Sauce
12oz (350g) closed cup
   mushrooms, sliced
1 clove garlic, crushed
1 teaspoon paprika
10½floz (300ml) beef stock
1 tablespoon redcurrant jelly
1 tablespoon tomato purée
2 teaspoons cornstarch
   (cornflour)
1 tablespoon water
2 tablespoons half and half
   (single) cream

Serves 4

- Heat the oil in a large frying pan. Season the pork steaks with pepper and fry for 1 minute on each side to brown, then cook for a further 5 minutes on each side, or until tender and cooked through. Remove and keep warm.
- To make the sauce, add the mushrooms and garlic to the frying pan and fry for 2 minutes, or until softened. Stir in the paprika, beef stock, redcurrant jelly and tomato purée. Bring to the boil, then simmer for 5 minutes or until reduced slightly.
- Mix the cornstarch with the water to form a paste, stir into the sauce and simmer for a further 2 minutes or until the sauce has thickened.
- Return the pork steaks to the pan, turn off the heat and stir in the cream. Season to taste and serve.

· RACK of VEAL · with THYME

1lb 10oz (750g) potatoes, peeled and cut into large dice

⅓ cup olive oil

1 tablespoon capers, chopped

2 tablespoons roasted garlic purée

salt and freshly ground black pepper

2lb 3oz (1kg) rack of veal (8 points)

8 sprigs thyme, leaves removed and stalks discarded

1¼ cups dry white wine

1¼ cups chicken stock

Serves 4

- Preheat the oven to 360°F (180°C).
- Boil the potatoes until soft. Drain, then mash or purée, and add half the olive oil, the chopped capers and 1 tablespoon roasted garlic purée. Mix well, season with salt and pepper, and set aside until ready to serve.
- Heat remaining olive oil in a pan and brown the veal on both sides, until well sealed (approximately 5 minutes). Remove the veal from the pan, and place on a rack in a baking dish. Rub with remaining roasted garlic purée and half the thyme, and season with salt and pepper. Add half the wine and stock to the baking dish.
- Roast in the oven for 20 minutes, or until veal is cooked to your liking. Wrap in foil and let rest for 10 minutes.
- Add remaining stock, wine and thyme to the pan juices and cook over a medium heat for 5 minutes, until the liquid has reduced by one-third.
- Serve veal on the mashed potato with pan juices, and garnish with extra sprig of thyme.

· BRAISED · LAMB SHANKS

2 tablespoons olive oil
4 lamb shanks
1 onion, chopped
1 clove garlic (optional),
  crushed
1 carrot, diced
½ cup celery, diced
1 cup canned diced tomatoes
1 teaspoon salt
¼ teaspoon freshly ground
  black pepper
½ teaspoon sugar
¼ cup beef stock or water
1 teaspoon Worcestershire
  sauce

Serves 4

- Heat oil in a frying pan and brown lamb shanks over a moderately high heat. Pour off most of the oil and reduce heat. Add onion, garlic (if used), carrot and celery, and cook until onion is soft. Stir in tomatoes, salt, pepper, sugar, stock and Worcestershire sauce.
- Spoon some of the vegetable mixture over the shanks. Place a lid on the pan and simmer for 2 hours, or until tender. Adjust flavour before serving.
- Serve with mashed potatoes and steamed vegetables.

MEATLOAF

1½lb (750g) ground
  (minced) beef
1½oz (45g) breadcrumbs
1 onion, grated
½ cup carrot, grated
2 tablespoons capsicum (red
  pepper), finely chopped
¼ cup tomato purée
¼ cup milk
1 egg, beaten
2 tablespoons parsley,
  chopped
½ teaspoon mixed herbs
1½ teaspoons salt
freshly ground black pepper,
  to taste
chopped parsley, to garnish

Serves 4–6

- Preheat oven to 350°F (180°C). Place minced beef in a large bowl. In another bowl, blend together the breadcrumbs, onion, carrot, capsicum (if used), tomato purée and milk. Stir in egg, herbs and salt and pepper. Combine this mixture with the minced beef.
- Spoon meat mixture into a greased standard-sized loaf tin and bake in the oven for 1 hour.
- Drain off liquid, unmould onto a warm serving platter and serve garnished with parsley and accompanied by steamed vegetables and potatoes.

- VARIATION Tomato–Cheese Loaf: Unmould meatloaf as above, lay slices of tomato and cheese on top, and return to the oven until cheese melts and browns slightly.

POTATO AND TOMATO PIE

3 cups vegetable stock
1lb 10oz (750g) potatoes,
  peeled and thinly sliced
1 red capsicum (pepper)
6 Roma tomatoes, sliced
2 tablespoons lemon juice
2 tablespoons olive oil
¼ teaspoon sugar
freshly ground black pepper
¼ small bunch flat-leaf
  parsley, chopped
¼ small bunch cilantro
  (coriander), chopped

Serves 4

- Heat vegetable stock in a large frying pan over medium heat. Add potatoes and cook for 8–10 minutes or until tender. Drain potatoes, reserving ½ cup stock, and rinse under cold water.
- Cut pepper into four and remove seeds. Place on a baking tray and bake under a hot grill for 6-8 minutes or until skin blisters. Leave to cool then remove skin and slice thinly.
- Preheat oven to 430°F (220°C) and lightly butter a shallow casserole dish. Arrange potato slices and pepper in the casserole dish. Pour over reserved stock and arrange tomato slices on top. Drizzle with lemon juice and olive oil, then sprinkle with sugar and season with pepper.
- Bake for 20 minutes or until tomatoes are cooked. Garnish with parsley and cilantro to serve.

- NOTE Suitable for vegetarians, vegans and wheat allergy sufferers.

LAMB CUTLETS WITH GARLIC MASH

12 lamb cutlets or loin
  chops
1 tablespoon lemon juice
1 tablespoon oil
salt to taste
1 teaspoon dried oregano
dash of black pepper

Garlic mash
1 teaspoon oil
1 large onion, finely diced
2 teaspoons freshly crushed
  garlic
1lb 10oz (750g) potatoes,
  peeled and cut into even
  sized pieces
½ cup milk
1 tablespoon butter
2 tablespoons grated
  Parmesan cheese
caramelized onion
small bunch of arugula
  (rocket), to serve

Redcurrant sauce
¼ cup redcurrant jelly
1 tbsp red wine or water

Serves 3–4

- Place lamb cutlets on a platter. Whisk the lemon juice, oil, oregano leaves and salt together. Brush onto both sides of the cutlets. Grind pepper onto both sides. Stand at room temperature for 30 minutes.
- Meanwhile, prepare the mash. Place the potatoes on to boil. Heat oil in a small pan, add onions and stir to coat well with oil. Reduce heat to low, cover with a lid and cook 6 minutes to soften the onions. Remove lid, increase heat, add garlic, and stir continuously until onions are a rich golden shade.
- When potatoes are tender, drain and mash with the milk and butter. Stir in the onion garlic mixture and Parmesan cheese. Keep hot.
- Heat the grill to hot, spray surface with oil spray. Place on the cutlets and cook for 2 to 3 minutes each side, or to your liking, brushing frequently with any remaining oil lemon mixture. Meanwhile, heat the redcurrant jelly with the red wine or water, until it is runny.
- To serve, place a mound of garlic mash on each plate. Place 3 to 4 cutlets on top, drizze with sauce and garnish with arugula leaves.

· BASIC PIE ·

17½oz (500g) very lean
  ground (minced) beef
1 medium onion, finely
  chopped
salt and freshly ground black
  pepper to taste
1 teaspoon mixed chopped
  fresh herbs
1 cup water
2 tablespoons all-purpose
  (plain) flour, mixed to a
  paste with water
2 sheets shortcrust pastry
1 egg, whisked

Serves 4

○ First, prepare the filling. Place the beef, half the onion, salt and pepper, mixed herbs and water, into a saucepan and bring to the boil.

○ Reduce the heat to a simmer, cover the saucepan and cook for 30 minutes.

○ Add the rest of the onion and thicken with the flour mixture. Add the flour mixture to the beef a little at a time until thickened. Adjust seasonings if necessary.

○ Preheat oven to 400°F (200°C) and lightly grease four ovenproof ramekins. Cut four rounds out of the pastry to form the base of each pie and fit these into the ramekins. Divide mixture evenly, spooning ⅓ cup of filling into each pie.

○ Cut smaller rounds of pastry for the tops, and carefully position these over the pies. Trim the edges and secure pastry by pressing edges down firmly, using a fork. Brush pastry with egg. Bake for 30 minutes, or until golden.

· BACON AND EGG PIE ·

2 sheets puff pastry
1 medium brown onion
   (approximately 1 cup),
   finely chopped
4oz (125g) bacon, diced
2 tablespoons spicy chutney
6 medium eggs
salt and pepper
1 tablespoon milk

Serves 6

- Preheat oven to 400°F (200°C) and lightly grease an 8in (20cm) square ovenproof dish. Line the dish with 1 sheet of pastry.
- Sprinkle onion and bacon evenly over the pastry, then dot the chutney on top. Break eggs evenly over the top, pricking the yolks so they run slightly. Season with salt and pepper.
- Carefully position second sheet of pastry over filling, trim edges, and secure pastry by pressing down edges firmly using a fork. Brush pastry with milk.
- Bake for 40 minutes or until risen and golden. Serve hot or cold with grilled vine-ripened cherry tomatoes and a leafy green salad.

- NOTE If you prefer, you can use chopped baby spinach instead of bacon in this recipe.

· TOMATO EGG PIE ·

1 sheet shortcrust pastry
4 tomatoes, sliced
salt and freshly ground black
  pepper
¼ cup fresh basil, chopped
3 eggs
½ cup half and half (single)
  cream
¼ cup yogurt
2 tablespoons Parmesan
  cheese, grated
1 tablespoon butter, cubed,
  extra

Serves 6

○ Line a 10in (25cm) flan tin with shortcrust pastry. Prick the pastry case with a fork, line with baking paper and half-fill with uncooked rice. Bake for 8 minutes, then remove rice or beans and paper, and bake for 10 minutes longer or until pastry is golden.
○ Arrange tomatoes in one layer in the cooked pastry shell. Season with salt and pepper to taste, and sprinkle on basil.
○ Combine eggs with cream and yogurt, pour gently over tomatoes, sprinkle on Parmesan cheese and dot with butter.
○ Bake in oven for 25 minutes or until top is golden and eggs have set. Let cool slightly and serve.

CHICKEN AND LEEK PIE

1 sheet shortcrust pastry
2 medium leeks, washed and
   sliced
2oz (60g) butter
1 tablespoon oil
13oz (375g) chicken,
   chopped finely
3 leaves sage, finely chopped
salt and freshly ground black
   pepper to taste
¾ cup Gruyère or Jarlsberg
   cheese, grated
⅔ cup half and half (single)
   cream
2 eggs

Serves 6-8

○ Preheat oven to 400°F (200°C). Line a 9in (23cm) pie plate with pastry. Prick the bottom of the pastry shell with a fork and refrigerate the shell for 1 hour.

○ Line the shell with baking paper and half-fill with rice. Bake for 10 minutes. Remove paper and rice and bake the shell for a further 10–15 minutes or until it is lightly colored. Remove from oven and allow to cool. Reduce oven heat to 360°F (180°C).

○ In a saucepan, over low heat, sauté the leeks in butter and oil for 15 minutes or until the leeks are soft. Add the chicken meat and cook for a further 5 minutes.

○ Stir in sage and seasonings. Allow mixture to cool. Beat the cream and egg together. Sprinkle ½ cup cheese on base of shell, add the chicken mixture and pour over egg mixture. Sprinkle with remaining cheese and bake for 35 minutes. Cut into slices and serve.

IRISH STEW

3 carrots, thinly sliced
2 onions, thinly sliced
17½oz (500g) potatoes,
   thinly sliced
8 lamb neck chops
salt and freshly ground black
   pepper
2 bay leaves
2 cups chicken stock,
   simmering

Serves 4

- If using a slow cooker, put all the vegetables into it. Trim the chops of any excess fat and lay these on top of the vegetables. Add the seasoning, bay leaves and stock. Cover and cook for 6–8 hours on high, or 10–14 hours on low.
- If cooking on the stove, sauté the onion in oil for 5 minutes, or until soft, in a saucepan over low heat. Add the carrots and potatos and cook for a further 10 minutes.
- Trim the fat off the chops and add to the pan, cooking for 5 minutes until sealed. Add the seasoning and bay leaves, cooking for 1 minute, and then add the chicken stock. Continue cooking for 2–3 hours on a low heat, stirring occasionally, adding extra stock or water as required.
- Serve hot, with warm, crusty bread.

TRADITIONAL LASAGNE

24 instant lasagne sheets
  (no pre-cooking required)
2oz (60g) mozzarella
  cheese, grated

Cheese sauce
2½oz (75g) butter
⅓ cup all-purpose (plain)
  flour
2 cups milk
3oz (90g) Cheddar cheese,
  grated
freshly ground black pepper

Meat sauce
2 teaspoons vegetable oil
2 onions, chopped
2 cloves garlic, crushed
2lb 12oz (1.25kg) ground
  (minced) beef
2 x 14oz (400g) canned
  diced tomatoes
¾ cup red wine
2 tablespoons chopped
  mixed herbs
freshly ground black pepper

Serves 6

- To make cheese sauce, melt butter in a saucepan over a medium heat. Stir in flour and cook, stirring, for 1 minute. Remove pan from heat and whisk in milk. Return pan to heat and cook, stirring, for 4–5 minutes or until sauce boils and thickens. Stir in cheese and black pepper to taste and set aside.
- Preheat the oven to 360°F (180°C). To make meat sauce, heat oil in a skillet over a medium heat. Add onions and garlic and cook, stirring, for 3 minutes or until onions are soft. Add beef and cook, stirring, for 5 minutes or until beef is brown. Stir in tomatoes, wine and herbs, bring to simmering point and simmer, stirring occasionally, for 15 minutes or until sauce in reduced and thickened. Season to taste with black pepper.
- Line the base of a large greased baking dish with 6 lasagne sheets. Top with one-quarter of the meat sauce and one-quarter of the cheese sauce. Repeat layers to use all ingredients, ending with a layer of cheese sauce.
- Sprinkle top of lasagne with mozzarella cheese and bake for 30–40 minutes or until it is hot and bubbling and the top is golden.

SPAGHETTI BOLOGNESE

400g spaghetti
2oz (60g) Parmesan, grated

Sauce
1 tablespoon olive oil
1 medium onion, finely
  chopped
1 carrot, finely diced
1 stalk celery, finely diced
2 cloves garlic, finely
  chopped
9oz (250g) ground (minced)
  beef steak
2 x 14oz (400g) canned
  diced tomatoes
1 bay leaf
2 teaspoons dried oregano
1 teaspoon sugar
salt and freshly ground black
  pepper
1/3 cup red wine

Serves 4

- To make the sauce, put the oil in a medium-sized heavy-based saucepan and heat over a medium heat. Add the onion, carrot, celery and garlic and cook, stirring, for 5 minutes or until the vegetables have softened.
- Add the beef to the pan, breaking it up into smaller pieces with a wooden spoon. Cook for 10 minutes or until the meat has browned.
- Stir in the tomatoes, bay leaf, oregano, sugar and salt and pepper, then pour in the red wine. Bring to the boil and stir well, then reduce the heat to low, cover, and cook for 20–25 minutes until thickened. Stir the sauce from time to time.
- While the sauce is cooking, bring a large saucepan of salted water to the boil, add the pasta and cook for 8 minutes or until just firm in the center.
- Drain the spaghetti in a colander. Remove the bay leaf from the sauce. Serve the pasta in a large shallow bowl with the sauce poured over and sprinkled with Parmesan.

· FRESH PASTA · WITH TOMATO SAUCE

17½oz (500g) fresh pasta

Sauce
2 tablespoons olive oil
1 medium onion, chopped
2 cloves garlic, chopped
2 x 14oz (400g) canned
   chopped tomatoes
1 teaspoon sugar
1 bay leaf
salt and freshly ground black
   pepper

Serves 4

○ To make the sauce, heat the oil in a medium-sized heavy-based saucepan over a medium heat. Add the onion and cook, stirring from time to time, for 2 minutes or until the onions are slightly softened. Add the garlic and cook, stirring occasionally, for 3 minutes or until the onion is tender.

○ Add the tomatoes to the pan with the sugar and bay leaf. Bring to the boil and season with salt and pepper. Reduce the heat, partly cover the pan and simmer, stirring occasionally, for 20 minutes, until the sauce has thickened. Remove the bay leaf.

○ Meanwhile, bring a large saucepan of salted water to the boil, add the pasta and cook for 2–3 minutes or until just firm in the center (*al dente*). Drain and serve with the sauce poured over.

○ NOTE It is possible to vary this recipe by stirring one of the following into the sauce, and cooking for 1 minute to heat through: 7oz (200g) canned tuna, drained and flaked; a handful of fresh basil leaves, roughly torn into pieces; 1–2 tablespoons of capers, drained and rinsed, and 10 pitted black olives, halved; or 1 red chilli, deseeded and chopped and 3 bacon rashers, grilled and crumbled into pieces.

PRESERVED DUCK AND PORK CASSEROLE

2lb (1kg) small dried white
beans, soaked overnight
1 teaspoon dried thyme,
leaves, picked and stalks
removed
2 onions, peeled and halved,
each half stuck with a
clove
1 bay leaf
1 bulb garlic, halved
crosswise
2 ham hocks
salt and freshly ground black
pepper
6 legs of confit duck
2 tablespoons fat
1 onion, coarsely chopped
1 tablespoon garlic, minced
2lb (1kg) garlic pork
sausages, cut into 2in
(5cm) chunks

Serves 6

- Drain beans and place in a large stockpot. Add thyme, onion halves, bay leaf, garlic bulb, ham hocks and black pepper. Add cold water to cover by 1¼in (3cm). Bring to a simmer over moderately high heat. Reduce heat to low and cook for 2 hours, adding water as necessary to keep beans barely covered.
- Taste beans and add salt if necessary. Remove onion halves and garlic bulb. Strip meat from the ham hocks in large chunks. Transfer beans, bay leaf, and ham to a large earthenware casserole.
- Bring duck legs to room temperature, letting excess fat drip off. Wipe duck legs with paper towel.
- Preheat oven to 300°F (150°C). In a medium skillet over low heat, melt 2 tablespoons fat. Add chopped onion and minced garlic and sauté for 10 minutes. Add to beans, along with sausage and duck legs.
- Cover loosely with foil and bake for 1¼ hours. Uncover and bake for 30 minutes more. Serve direct from the casserole dish.

THE CLASSIC ROASTS WITH SIDES

...

THE CLASSIC ROASTS WITH SIDES

∘∘∘

Who doesn't remember roast dinners growing up? Whether it was every week at Nanna's house, or reserved for special occasions, a roast was always a highly anticipated event. The house filled up with the delicious smells of cooking meat and vegetables. Everyone had their favourite sides, the recipes of which were often closely-guarded family secrets. When the meat came out on a silver platter, followed by all the trimmings, it was a truly magical moment.

Nothing has changed today – most of us adore a roast and it is still an exciting family event. In this chapter, we have featured the traditional roast dinners, along with all the classic sides, so that you can recreate that childhood magic.

∘ TIPS FOR BEEF ∘

Topside/top loin or rib are typical cuts. The meat should have a thick layer of fat to start with, which will stop it from drying out while it's cooking. Rest the meat for at least 15 minutes once it's done, and slice it thinly. Serve with gravy, horseradish and Yorkshire puddings, for real authenticity!

∘ TIPS FOR CHICKEN ∘

Buy a free-range chicken, widely available these days. Lemon is often rubbed on the chicken before roasting, along with salt and pepper, or stuffed inside it. Season to your own taste.

You may like to start with the chicken breast-side down; when you turn it over, halfway through cooking, the juices will move through the roast nicely. Rest the roasted chicken for at least 15 minutes when it's done. It should have golden, crispy skin, but juicy, tender meat.

∘ TIPS FOR LAMB ∘

Roast lamb is naturally popular in the spring. The best cuts for roasting are leg, shoulder, saddle and loin.

Before cooking, allow the meat to reach room temperature, and season well, remembering that lamb goes hand in hand with rosemary. It should be served pink and tender, but the time it takes to cook will depend on the cut and the weight. Ask your butcher if in doubt.

๏ TIPS FOR PORK ๏

Try roasting spare rib, blade (boned and rolled by the butcher), loin or leg joint. It can be tricky to get that much-loved crackling just right – to do so, ensure the skin is very dry before cooking; score the skin, which will allow the fat below to rise to the surface; and sprinkle with plenty of salt.

Pork should not be at all pink when cooked. To check, poke it with a skewer. If juices are clear and not pink, it is likely ready to eat.

๏ SAUCES ๏

Gravies and other sauces can be made with the pan juices from your roast meat. Some traditional taste combinations should be considered – a lamb is served with mint jelly, while pork typically needs apple sauce and turkey is best with cranberry.

You might like to prepare your own sauces in advance (see pages 171–193).

ROAST CHICKEN

3lb 15oz (1.8kg) chicken
finely grated zest and juice
  of 2 lemons
2 cloves garlic, crushed
salt and freshly ground black
  pepper
2 teaspoons chopped fresh
  oregano
2 tablespoons olive oil

Sides
4 medium potatoes, peeled
  and quartered
17½oz (500g) pumpkin
  cut into portions (skin on)
pared lemon zest and lemon
  wedges to garnish
sprigs of oregano to garnish

Serves 6

- Wash chicken inside and out, drain, then pat dry with absorbent paper. Mix together half of the lemon zest, lemon juice, garlic, salt, pepper, oregano and oil.
- Stand the chicken in an oven tray and spoon half of the lemon mixture over the chicken and cavity. Place remaining zest in the cavity.
- Place chicken in the oven and cook for approximately 1¾ hours (around 30 minutes for every 1lb 2oz [500g] of chicken).
- About 1 hour before serving, place potatoes and pumpkin in 2 foil trays. Sprinkle with remaining lemon mixture, tossing around to coat all pieces. Cook for around 45 minutes, or more if the pieces are large and will take time to cook.
- Remove vegetables and chicken when cooked. Cover to keep hot and rest chicken before carving.
- Garnish with lemon zest, lemon wedges and sprigs of oregano. Serve hot with roasted vegetables.

SWEET POTATOES WITH SAGE

2lb 3oz (1kg) orange sweet
   potatoes, peeled and cut
   into even-size pieces
1oz (30g) butter
2 tablespoon vegetable oil
1½ tablespoon honey
pinch of ground ginger
6 fresh sage leaves torn into
   pieces

Serves 8

- Preheat oven to 360°F (180°C). Cook sweet potatoes in a large saucepan of boiling salted water for 5 minutes. Drain.
- Melt the butter with the oil in a baking dish and stir in honey and ginger. Add the sage and the sweet potatoes and toss in mixture to coat.
- Bake for 40 minutes, brushing with honey mixture and turning occasionally, until potatoes are tender. Garnish with extra sage.

- NOTE Sweet potatoes are often known as yams in the US and Canada, even though the genuine yam, an edible tuber very popular in Africa, is quite different.

MINTED PEAS

4 cups fresh or frozen peas
5 whole sprigs mint, plus
5 sprigs with stalks removed
  and leaves shredded
1½oz (40g) butter
salt
white pepper

Serves 6

- Place the peas in a saucepan and pour in enough water to just cover. Add the whole mint sprigs. Bring to the boil and simmer for 5 minutes if fresh, 2 minutes if frozen.
- Meanwhile, in a small saucepan over a low heat, melt the butter and add the shredded mint to infuse.
- When the peas are cooked, drain and discard the mint. Return peas to the saucepan, add the butter and shredded mint, and stir over a low heat until combined. Season with salt and white pepper.

LEG OF LAMB WITH VEGETABLES

1 leg of lamb (about 3lb
  5oz, or 1½kg)
2 cloves garlic, cut into
  slivers
2 fresh rosemary sprigs, cut
  into small pieces
salt and black pepper
14oz (400g) parsnips,
  chopped
10½oz (300g) carrots,
  chopped
6 heads chicory (curly
  endive) cut into quarters
  lengthwise
1¼ cups red wine
2 tablespoons red wine
  vinegar

Serves 4

- Preheat the oven to 360°F (180°C). Make several incisions in the lamb using a sharp knife. Push the garlic slivers and pieces of rosemary into the incisions, then season well.
- Arrange the parsnips, carrots and chicory in a large roasting tin and place the lamb on top. Pour in the wine and vinegar and roast for 2–2½ hours until the lamb is tender, basting the lamb and turning the vegetables in the cooking juices every 30 minutes. Add a little more wine or water if necessary.
- Transfer the lamb to a plate, reserving the cooking juices, then cover with foil and rest for 15 minutes. Carve the lamb and serve with the vegetables, with the cooking juices drizzled over.

SPICED RED CABBAGE

1lb 10oz (750g) red
  cabbage
1 large red onion, chopped
1 green apple, cored and
  chopped
2 cloves garlic, crushed
¼ teaspoon ground cloves
¼ teaspoon ground nutmeg
1½ tablespoons Demerara
  (raw) sugar
2 tablespoons red wine
  vinegar
¾oz (20g) butter, cut into
  ½in (1cm) cubes
salt and freshly ground
  black pepper

Serves 6

- Preheat the oven to 300°F (150°C). Cut the cabbage into quarters and remove the white core. Finely slice the leaves and add to a large ovenproof dish, then add the onion and apple and toss to combine.
- In a small bowl, combine the garlic, spices, sugar and vinegar. Pour the mixture over the cabbage, and toss to combine again. Distribute the butter cubes across the top evenly.
- Cover and bake for 1½ hours, stirring once after the first hour. Season and serve hot.

LAMB RACKS with EGGPLANT MASH

4 large eggplants (aubergine)
10½oz (300g) potatoes,
  peeled and coarsely
  chopped
4 racks of lamb, French
  trimmed, about 9oz
  (250g) each
¼ cup dukkah

Serves 4

- Preheat the grill to high, and preheat the oven to 375°F (190°C).
- Prick the eggplants with a fork, then place on a baking tray. Grill, turning occasionally, for 15 minutes until skin has blackened and insides are tender. Remove and set aside to cool. Cut the eggplants in half lengthwise. Scoop the flesh out into a medium bowl and mash with a fork. Set aside and keep warm.
- Meanwhile, place the potatoes in a medium saucepan. Cover with cold water and bring to the boil. Cook for 5–10 minutes or until tender. Drain, return to the saucepan and mash. Add the eggplant and stir to combine.
- Coat the lamb in dukkah and roast for 25 minutes for medium or until cooked to your liking. Transfer to a plate, cover and rest for 5 minutes. Serve with smoky mash.

- NOTE Dukkah is an Egyptian dry spice mixture of chopped nuts and seeds. It's available at specialty food stores.

CAULIFLOWER CHEESE

17½oz (500g) cauliflower,
  cut into small pieces
¼ cup fresh breadcrumbs
¼ small bunch flat-leaf
  parsley

Cheese sauce
1oz (30g) butter
¼ cup all-purpose (plain)
  flour
1¼ cups milk, warmed
1 teaspoon wholegrain
  mustard
2½oz (80g) Parmesan
  cheese, grated, at room
  temperature
salt
white pepper

Serves 4

- Lightly butter a heatproof dish. Cook the cauliflower in a saucepan of lightly salted boiling water for 8 minutes or until just tender. Drain thoroughly, then transfer to the prepared dish and keep warm.
- To make the cheese sauce, melt the butter in a pan over low heat. Stir in the flour and cook for 1 minute, or until lightly colored and bubbling. Remove from the heat and gradually stir in the milk and mustard. If lumps form, press the mixture through a strainer. Return to the heat and stir constantly until the sauce simmers and thickens. Reduce the heat and simmer for a further 2 minutes, then remove from the heat again.
- Add the Parmesan and stir until thoroughly combined. Season with salt and white pepper and pour over the cauliflower.
- Combine the breadcrumbs and parsley and sprinkle evenly on top of the sauce. Grill under a medium heat until the top is golden brown. Serve immediately.

· TOMATO RIB ROAST ·

6-point standing rib roast
   of beef, about 3lb 5oz
   (1½kg)
salt and freshly ground black
   pepper
2 cloves garlic, crushed
2 tablespoons all-purpose
   (plain) flour

Tomato sauce
8 Roma tomatoes, finely
   chopped
1 medium red onion, finely
   chopped
10 leaves basil, chopped
sprinkle of garlic bread
   seasoning
salt
1 tablespoon olive oil
1½ tablespoons balsamic
   dressing

Serves 6

- Preheat oven to 400°F (200°C). Rub the roast with salt, pepper and crushed garlic. Just before placing in the oven, dust all over with flour – this helps to seal in the juices. Place in the oven and cook for 50 minutes until medium rare (cook for a further 15 minutes for well done).
- Meanwhile, combine all tomato sauce ingredients in a small saucepan ready for heating. Remove the roast from the oven and rest the meat for 5 minutes. Warm the sauce while the meat rests.

YORKSHIRE PUDDINGS

4 eggs
¾ cup milk
2 cups all-purpose (plain) flour
1 teaspoon salt
¼ small bunch parsley, chopped
¼ small bunch chives, chopped
½ cup vegetable oil

Serves 4

◦ Combine the eggs and milk thoroughly with a fork (do not whisk). Then, using a whisk to combine, add enough of the flour to form a thick but pourable batter. Add salt to taste, then the chopped herbs.

◦ Preheat oven to 400°F (200°C). In a 12-cup muffin tray, add 2 teaspoons of oil to each muffin section, and place in the oven for 15 minutes. When both the tray and the oil are hot, pour in the batter – if it does not start to sizzle immediately, stop and return tray to the oven until it's hot enough.

◦ Place on the middle shelf and bake for about 25 minutes until risen, golden brown and slightly crisp – an empty tray on the top shelf will help prevent them browning too much. Remove from the oven, carefully remove muffins from the tray, and serve immediately.

◦ NOTE Recipes for Yorkshire pudding were first published in England in the 18th century, and this ancient batter-based treat remains an essential staple of English roast dinners today.

ROAST BEEF WITH POTATO CAKES

2lb 12oz (1⅓kg) standing
 rib roast of beef
salt and pepper
2 teaspoons crushed garlic
2 tablespoons all-purpose
 (plain) flour
10oz (285g) jar tomato
 salsa

Potato cakes
4 medium-sized potatoes,
 boiled in their jackets
2oz (55g) eggs, lightly
 beaten
2 teaspoons Cajun
 seasoning
2 tablespoons olive oil
2 tablespoons all-purpose
 (plain) flour
½ teaspoon salt

Gravy
pan juices from roast meat
2–3 tablespoons plain flour
2 cups beef stock or water
salt and pepper, to taste

Serves 8

- Preheat the oven to 475°F (240°C).
- Rub the roast with salt, pepper and crushed garlic and stand at room temperature for 20 minutes. Just before placing on the barbecue, dust all over with flour. This helps to seal in the juices. Place the salsa in a small saucepan ready for heating and prepare the potato cake mixture.
- Place the beef on a roasting tray in the preheated oven. Turn the heat down to 400°F (200°C) and cook for 1 hour for medium. Remove from the oven, cover with foil and leave it stand for 20 minutes.
- To make the potato cakes, skin the boiled potatoes and mash well. Add the eggs, Cajun seasoning, olive oil, flour and salt. Mix well and form into 16 patties using floured hands. Cook in a pan for about 5 minutes on each side. Heat the salsa while the patties are cooking.
- Carve the roast and serve with the potato cakes and a tomato salsa or gravy.

Gravy
- After removing the roast from the baking tray, set aside about 1 cup of pan juices to make the gravy.
- Put pan juices in a saucepan over a medium heat and sprinkle over flour. Stir with a wooden spoon until mixture thickens. Add stock, stirring constantly, and simmer gently for 5–10 minutes. Add a little extra stock or water if necessary. Season with salt or pepper.

ROAST POTATOES GARLIC AND ROSEMARY

3lb 5oz (1½kg) chat
  potatoes
coarse sea salt
1 bulb garlic
6 sprigs rosemary, leaves
  removed and chopped
6 tablespoons olive oil

Serves 8

- Preheat oven to 375°F (190°C). Place potatoes in a saucepan, cover with water, add salt and bring to the boil. Reduce heat and simmer for 2 minutes, then drain well. Make a few cuts across the tops of the potatoes. Break open the garlic and discard any loose pieces of skin.
- Place potatoes and garlic cloves in a roasting dish, sprinkle with the chopped rosemary and oil. Bake for about 1¼ hours, turning occasionally, until crisp and golden brown.
- Transfer to a warmed serving dish, sprinkle with salt and garnish with extra rosemary sprigs.

ROAST RIB OF BEEF WITH HERBED SAUCE

6-point standing rib roast,
    about 3lb 5oz (1½ kg)
salt and freshly ground
    black pepper

Herbed sauce
6 scallions (spring onions),
    finely chopped
1 very small clove garlic,
    chopped
3 tablespoons dry white
    wine
1 tablespoon wine vinegar
9oz (250g) butter, at room
    temperature
¼ cup parsley, chopped
¼ cup chervil, chopped
1 teaspoon lemon juice
1 teaspoon salt
freshly ground black pepper
ground nutmeg

Serves 6

- Preheat oven to 400°F (200°C). Rub roast all over with salt and black pepper. Place on a rack, fat-side up, in a roasting dish and roast for 50 minutes.
- To make sauce, place scallions, garlic, wine and vinegar in a small saucepan. Bring to the boil and boil for 2 minutes or until reduced to 1 tablespoon. Cool slightly, then gradually whisk in butter until blended and creamy, like mayonnaise. Stir in herbs, lemon juice, salt, black pepper and nutmeg to taste. Place in a sauce boat and set in a pan of warm water to keep warm.
- To serve, place beef fat-side down on a carving board and remove ribs by cutting close down the line of bones. Cut ribs apart and set aside. Turn roast upright and carve slices from one end, arranging them around the roast for serving. Serve beef with the ribs, pan juices and sauce.

BROCCOLINI with ALMONDS

17½oz (500g) broccolini,
  stalks trimmed
2 teaspoons olive oil
¾oz (20g) butter
1 clove garlic, crushed
2 tablespoons flaked
  almonds

Serves 6

- Add the broccolini to a saucepan of boiling water and cook for 1–2 minutes, or until it is still just crunchy. Drain well.
- Heat the oil and butter in a large frying pan, add the garlic and almonds and cook for 1–2 minutes, or until the almonds are just golden. Remove the almonds from the pan with a slotted spoon and set aside.
- Add the broccolini to the frying pan and toss over medium heat for 2–3 minutes until the broccolini is heated through and well coated. Return the almonds to the pan and stir until well distributed. Serve hot.

ROAST PORK

3lb 5oz (1½kg) boned loin
  of pork
string for tying pork
1–2 tablespoons olive oil
salt

Stuffing
½ cup dried apricots, finely
  chopped
¼ cup macadamias, chopped
3 green onions, sliced
zest of 1 orange
1 teaspoon mixed herbs
¼ cup sage, chopped
¾ cup fresh breadcrumbs
1oz (30g) butter, melted

Serves 6

- Combine all stuffing ingredients in a bowl and set aside. Preheat the oven to 430°F (220°C).
- Score the pork rind with a sharp knife. Lay the pork fat-side down on a clean surface. Cut a slit into the pork, being careful not to cut all the way through. Spread the stuffing evenly over the pork and roll up. Tie with string at regular intervals.
- Place pork on a rack over a baking tray. Brush with olive oil and massage the salt into the skin.
- Bake for 20–30 minutes, reduce the heat to 360°F (180°C) and continue to cook for 1–1½ hours, or until cooked when tested with a skewer. Remove from the oven and cover with foil. Leave to stand for 15 minutes before slicing. Serve with roast potatoes and pumpkin.

BEER-GLAZED HAM

16lb 8oz (7½kg) leg
  of ham
40 cloves
2 cups stout beer, such as
  Guinness
1 cup soft brown sugar
2 tablespoons mustard
1 teaspoon ground ginger
2 teaspoons ground
  cardamom

Serves 20–30

- Preheat oven to 320°F (160°C). Remove the skin from the ham, leaving a portion of skin around the bone. Score the ham with diagonal lines in both directions and put a clove in the center of each section.
- Place ham fat-side up in a roasting dish and pour over 1¾ cups of the stout. Bake for 3 hours, basting occasionally with stout. Remove ham from oven and baste thoroughly.
- Increase oven temperature to 400°F (200°C). Combine sugar, mustard, ginger, cardamom and enough remaining stout to make a paste. Spread mixture over ham and bake for 35 minutes or until well glazed.

ROAST PORK with MUSTARD HERBS

2oz (60g) butter
2 teaspoons Dijon mustard
1 teaspoon mixed herbs
2lb 12oz (1.25kg) piece of
　pork scotch fillet
1½ tablespoons olive oil
2 teaspoons honey
½ teaspoon ginger, ground
1 bunch baby carrots, peeled
　and trimmed
3 parsnips, peeled and cut
　into wedges
1 tablespoon all-purpose
　(plain) flour
1½ cups beef stock

Serves 4

- Preheat the oven to 400°F (200°C).
- Combine half the butter, the Dijon mustard and mixed herbs in a bowl. Spread the mixture over the pork roast.
- Heat 2 teaspoons oil in a large frying pan over high heat. Sear the meat quickly until light golden all over. Remove the meat, leaving pan juices for gravy.
- Wrap the meat in foil and place on a rack over a baking tray. Bake in the oven for 1¼–1½ hours or until cooked.
- Meanwhile, heat the remaining oil and butter with the honey and ginger in a clean frying pan over low to medium heat. Sauté the carrots and parsnips for 10 minutes, turning from time to time.
- To make the gravy, add the flour to the pan juices and cook over low heat. Add the beef stock and stir until the mixture is smooth and thickens.
- Slice the meat and serve with sautéed carrots, parsnips and gravy.

FRESH
FROM THE
OVEN

...

FRESH FROM THE OVEN

○○○

With a co-operative oven and a touch of skill, anyone can whip up a creation that will dazzle guests, silence a mother-in-law and satisfy a grumbling belly. Whether it's a homemade loaf of bread, or a glorious tiered cake, these recipes are classic crowd-pleasers.

○ EQUIPMENT ○

Some mixing bowls, as well as a sieve, wooden spoon, rolling pin and whisk, will suffice for preparing most batters and doughs, though if you have an electric mixer, you may find it useful.

If you are in the market for cake tins, choose good-quality springform tins. Non-stick tins will give you years of faithful service if you treat them nicely, washing by hand and never cutting or scraping them with metal objects. Flat baking trays will do for bread and some pastries; pies and tarts will require dishes of the appropriate size and shape.

Quality scales and measuring cups are a necessity. Small, nested sets of cups are useful, as are tablespoon and teaspoon measures. For carefree ease of measuring, new digital scales can measure liquid as well as dry ingredients, in imperial and metric measurements.

○ A NOTE ON MEASUREMENTS ○

As is traditional in baking, for many ingredients, the recipes in this book use spoon and cup measurements. In some cases, for precision, measurements are given in oz and grams.

1 teaspoon = 5g = ¼oz = 5ml
1 tablespoon = 15g = ½oz = 15ml
Liquid measures: 1 cup = 9 fl oz (250ml).

Solid measures vary depending on the ingredient. For the following key ingredients, they are approximately as follows: 1 cup superfine (caster) sugar = 7oz (220g); 1 cup flour = 5oz (150g); 1 cup confectioners' (icing) sugar = 5oz (150g); 1 cup raisins = 5½oz (170g).

These conversions are rounded for cookery purposes.

৹ BAKING BREAD ৹

Making your own bread is easier than you might think. Once you've nailed your recipe, it can be a great addition to your weekly cooking routine, just as it was for the home cooks of the past. It may take a little practice to perfect your lovely loaves, but as long as you follow the directions and weigh or measure properly, it's hard to go too wrong.

Do remember that the moisture content (in the air around you and in the ingredients) makes a difference to the final product. It can be helpful to keep a record of your bread-baking attempts – for example, by noting down the ambient, water and dough temperatures – so that you will be able to replicate good results.

Pre-heating the oven for half an hour prior to baking is essential.

৹ BLIND BAKING ৹

Some pastry recipes call for 'blind baking'. This is a process of pre-baking the pastry case before it is filled. It's a necessary step when the filling isn't going to be baked, or when the filling takes less time to bake than the pastry. Blind baking lends other useful effects, such as preventing the crust from becoming soggy later, and helps to form a nice, firm case for the filling.

Instructions for blind baking are generally given in the relevant recipes. Recipes may advise the use of baking beans or uncooked rice; use what you prefer.

SODA BREAD

1⅓ cup all-purpose (plain) flour
1 teaspoon baking soda (bicarbonate of soda)
1 teaspoon salt
1½oz (45g) butter
2 cups buttermilk or milk

Serves 8

- Preheat oven to 400°F (200°C).
- Sift the flour, baking soda and salt into a bowl. Rub in the butter, using your fingertips, until the mixture resembles coarse breadcrumbs. Make a well in the center of the flour mixture, pour in the milk or buttermilk and, using a round-ended knife, mix to form a soft dough.
- Turn dough onto a floured surface and knead lightly until smooth. Shape into an 7in (18cm) round, and place on a buttered and floured baking tray. Score dough into eighths using a sharp knife. Dust lightly with flour and bake for 35–40 minutes, or until the loaf sounds hollow when tapped on the base.

COUNTRY CORNBREAD

1 cup cornmeal
1 cup all-purpose (plain)
  flour
2 tablespoons sugar
1 tablespoon baking powder
½ teaspoon salt
¾ cup milk
½ cup sour cream
2 eggs
3½oz (100g) butter, melted

Serves 8

- Preheat oven to 360°F (180°C).
- In a large mixing bowl, stir together all the dry ingredients. Mix the milk, cream, eggs and butter separately and blend well. Mix with the flour mixture until just combined.
- Pour the batter into a well-oiled square cake tin, about 9 x 9in (23 x 23cm). Bake for approximately 30 minutes, until a skewer inserted into the bread comes out clean. Cut into squares or rectangles and serve warm.

WHOLE WHEAT BREAD

1 cup whole wheat self-
rising (wholemeal self-
raising) flour
1 cup white self-rising
(self-raising) flour
1¼ cups non-fat (skim)
milk
1 teaspoon dry mustard
1 tablespoon sesame seeds

Serves 8

- Prehat oven to 400°F (200°C).
- Sift flour into a bowl, return husks from sifter to bowl. Stir in enough milk to give a sticky dough. Knead on lightly floured surface until smooth, shape into a round.
- Place dough onto lightly buttered oven tray, press out with fingers to about 1in (2.5cm) thick. Using a sharp knife, cut dough into wedges, cutting about ½in (1cm) deep.
- Sprinkle dough with combined mustard and sesame seeds. Bake for 30 minutes or until golden brown and hollow when tapped with fingers.

· HOLIDAY · SPICE BREAD

1oz (30g) unsalted butter, melted

1 cup almonds, coarsely chopped

½ cup raisins

¼ teaspoon salt

¼ teaspoon nutmeg

1 teaspoon ground ginger

1½ teaspoon ground cinnamon

1 teaspoon anise seed

pinch of ground cloves

1½ teaspoon dried orange peel, minced

1 teaspoon baking powder

2 teaspoons baking soda (bicarbonate of soda)

1 cup honey

¼ cup brown sugar

1 large egg, lightly beaten

⅓ cup dark rum

1 cup rye flour

1 cup whole wheat (wholemeal) flour

1 cup bread flour (strong plain flour)

Makes one loaf

○ Preheat oven to 400°F (200°C).

○ Butter one 8-cup loaf tin, 6 x 10in (5 x 25cm) or two 4½ cup loaf tins 3 x 7in (8 x 18cm). Dust bottom and sides with flour, shaking out excess.

○ In a large mixing bowl, combine almonds, raisins, salt, nutmeg, ginger, cinnamon, anise seed, cloves, orange peel, baking powder and baking soda.

○ Bring 1 cup water to a boil in a medium saucepan over moderate heat. Add honey and stir to dissolve. Add brown sugar and stir to dissolve. Remove from heat, allow to cool for 5 minutes.

○ Add egg and rum to honey and sugar mixture and whisk to blend. Add to spice mixture and stir to blend. Add flours and stir until flour is just absorbed (about 50 strokes). Transfer dough to prepared pan and bake for 10 minutes. Reduce heat to 360°F (180°C) and bake until a cake tester inserted in center comes out dry (about 30 more minutes for one large pan, 20–25 more minutes for smaller pans). Bread will be very dark.

○ Let bread cool in pan on a rack for 5 minutes. Remove from tin and finish cooling on rack. Wrap tightly with plastic wrap and store at room temperature for 2–3 days before serving. Thinly slice to serve.

· FRUITY · CARROT LOAF

1 cup whole wheat self-rising (wholemeal self-raising) flour
½ cup rye flour
½ cup Demerara (raw) sugar
½ teaspoon salt
½ tablespoon baking soda (bicarbonate of soda)
1 teaspoon ground cinnamon
½ cup crushed pineapple, undrained
1 cup grated carrot
2 eggs
½ cup oil
1 teaspoon vanilla extract
½ cup chopped walnuts

Lemon glacé topping
1 cup confectioners' (icing) sugar
1 teaspoon butter
few drops of vanilla extract
1 tablespoon lemon juice
½ teaspoon lemon zest

Makes 1 loaf

- Preheat oven to 360°F (180°C).
- Butter an 8 x 6in (20 x 15cm) loaf tin with melted butter or margarine and line the base with buttered baking paper.
- Sift the flours, sugar, salt, baking soda and cinnamon into a mixing bowl. Add the crushed pineapple, carrot, eggs, oil and vanilla and beat until well combined. Stir the chopped walnuts into the carrot mixture. Spoon the batter into prepared loaf tin. Bake for 25–30 minutes or until a skewer inserted in the center comes out clean.
- Remove from the oven and allow to cool in the tin for 5 minutes before turning out onto a wire rack to cool completely.
- To make lemon glacé topping, place sifted confectioners' sugar in a heat-proof bowl over a pan of simmering water. Make a well in the center of confectioners' sugar, add butter, vanilla extract and 1 tablespoon of lemon juice, and stir slowly until all confectioners' sugar has been incorporated and topping is smooth and shiny. Use while still warm.

CHERRY ALMOND CAKE

8oz (250g) butter or margarine
1 cup superfine (caster) sugar
2 eggs
2 cups all-purpose (plain) flour
½ teaspoon ground cinnamon
½ teaspoon ground cloves
8oz (250g) ground almonds
1 tablespoon gin
5 tablespoons cherry jam
1 cup whipped cream

Serves 12

- Preheat oven to 360°F (180°C).
- Beat butter until soft, add sugar and continue beating until light and fluffy. Add eggs one at a time, beating well after each addition.
- Sift flour, cinnamon, cloves and ground almonds together. Add to creamed mixture with gin, mixing with a wooden spoon until ingredients are well combined.
- Spoon half the cake mixture into a 8in (20cm) round deep cake tin that has been lined with buttered baking paper. Spread evenly with 3 tablespoons of the jam, then spread with remaining cake mixture.
- Bake for 1 hour or until pale golden. Cool in the tin for 5 minutes, then turn out onto a wire rack to cool. Spread top of cake with cream and decorate with remaining jam.

LEMON MERINGUE TART

Base pastry

5oz (150g) butter
⅓ cup superfine (caster)
 sugar
½ teaspoon vanilla extract
1 small egg
2 cups all-purpose (plain)
 flour
½ teaspoon baking powder
pinch salt

Lemon meringue

4 tablespoons cornstarch
 (cornflour)
¾ cup sugar
juice of ½ lemon
2 egg yolks
2 tablespoons butter,
 softened
grated zest of 1 lemon
3 egg whites
⅓ cup sugar

Serves 6–8

Preheat oven to 400°F (200°C). To make the pastry, sift together flour and baking powder. Cream the butter and sugar with the vanilla until light and fluffy. Add the egg. Fold the flour mixture into the creamed butter mixture.

Knead lightly until smooth, cover and refrigerate for about 30 minutes before using. Line a buttered 9in (23cm) pie plate with the pastry, decorate the edge and prick the bottom with a fork. Line pastry with baking paper and half-fill with rice and bake. Remove paper and rice and turn out case to cool. Reduce oven temperature to 360°F (180°C).

To make the lemon meringue, blend the cornstarch and sugar with 1 cup of water, lemon juice and egg yolks. Stir over low heat until the mixture boils and thickens. Beat in the butter and grated lemon zest. Allow to cool and pour into the pastry case.

Beat egg whites until stiff, gradually add the sugar and continue beating until thick and glossy. Pipe over the top of lemon filling and bake in the center of the oven until the meringue is firm and lightly browned.

APPLE AND COCONUT TART

Shortcrust pastry for
  9in (23cm) tin

Filling
4 teaspoons gelatin
1 cup canned apple purée
1 tablespoon superfine
  (caster) sugar
½ cup cream
2 egg whites

Topping
¼ cup apple purée
½ cup coconut
¼ cup brown sugar
½ cup cream

Serves 12

- Add the gelatin to ¼ cup hot water and stir briskly with a fork until dissolved. Add to the apple purée.
- Whisk the egg whites until stiff, continue whisking and gradually add the superfine sugar to form a meringue. Fold the cream and meringue into the gelatin/apple mixture. Pour into the pastry shell. Refrigerate until set.
- To make the topping, spread the apple purée over the top of the tart. Sprinkle the combined coconut and brown sugar over the apple. Whip cream and pipe around the edge.

HAZELNUT SHORTBREADS

9oz (250g) butter, chopped
1½ cups all-purpose (plain) flour, sifted
1½oz (45g) hazelnuts, ground
¼ cup ground rice
¼ cup superfine (caster) sugar
3½oz (100g) chocolate, melted

Makes 40

- Preheat oven to 320°F (160°C).
- Place butter, flour, hazelnuts and ground rice in a food processor and process until mixture resembles coarse breadcrumbs. Add sugar and process again to combine.
- Turn mixture onto a floured surface and knead lightly to make a pliable dough. Place dough between sheets of baking paper and roll out to ¼in (5mm) thick. Using a 2in (5cm) fluted cutter, cut out rounds of dough and place 1in (2.5cm) apart on buttered baking trays. Bake for 10–15 minutes or until lightly browned. Stand on baking trays for 2–3 minutes before transferring to wire racks to cool.
- Place melted chocolate in a plastic food bag, snip off one corner and pipe lines across each shortbread before serving.

HONEY NUT SHORTBREADS

½ cup any white nut, such
  as macadamia or cashew
1 cup all-purpose (plain)
  flour
½ cup cornstarch (cornflour)
¼ teaspoon salt
¼ cup superfine (caster)
  sugar
4oz (125g) butter
2 tablespoons honey

Makes 24

- Preheat oven to 400°F (200°C).
- Finely chop half the nuts. Cut the remainder in half and put aside.
- Sift flours, salt and sugar together. Rub in the butter until evenly dispersed, stir in the honey and chopped nuts.
- Turn onto a lightly floured board and knead lightly. Roll out to ½in (1cm) thickness and place in the refrigerator for about 10 minutes before cutting into rounds using a 2in (5cm) fluted cutter. Place half a nut on each round.
- Place the shortbreads on a buttered baking tray and bake in the oven for about 15 minutes, or until golden brown.

STRAWBERRY SHORTBREADS

8oz (250g) butter
½ cup superfine (caster)
  sugar
2 eggs, lightly beaten
1 teaspoon vanilla extract
1½ cups all-purpose (plain)
  flour
½ cup cornstarch (cornflour)
1 tablespoon baking powder

Strawberry cream
1 cup milk
½ teaspoon vanilla extract
⅓ cup superfine (caster)
  sugar
3 egg yolks
2 tablespoons cornstarch
  (cornflour)
¾ cup semi-whipped cream
1 cup sliced strawberries

Makes 1 cake

- Preheat oven 360°F (180°C).
- Cream the butter and sugar until light and fluffy, add the eggs and vanilla and beat thoroughly. Sift together the flour, cornstarch and baking powder. Fold into the egg mixture and combine well. Place into three buttered 7in (18cm) sandwich tins and bake in the center of the oven for 20 minutes. Allow to cool.
- To make the strawberry cream, first heat milk and vanilla in a heavy-based saucepan until boiling.
- Beat the sugar and eggs together in a bowl until the mixture is thick and creamy, and leaves a distinct trail when the beaters are lifted out of the mixture. Fold in the cornstarch. Then pour the hot milk onto the egg mixture, beating well.
- Return the mixture to the pan and reheat, stirring constantly. Boil for 1 minute, then pour into a bowl and cover with a sheet of baking paper. When cool, combine with whipped cream and strawberries.
- Fill the cake with the strawberry cream and decorate the top with extra whipped cream and strawberries.

CINNAMON ALMOND COOKIES

1½oz (45g) butter, at room
  temperature
½ cup sugar, plus
  2 extra tablespoons
4 tablespoons Amaretto
1 egg
2 cups all-purpose (plain)
  flour
1½ tablespoons instant
  coffee
2 teaspoons ground
  cinnamon

Makes 18

- Preheat oven to 375°F (190°C).
- Cream the butter and ½ cup of the sugar in a large bowl until light and fluffy. Add the Amaretto and egg and mix well.
- In a small bowl, whisk together the flour, coffee and 1 teaspoon of the cinnamon. Slowly mix the flour mixture into the butter mixture until thoroughly combined.
- In a small bowl, combine the 2 tablespoons sugar and the remaining cinnamon. Shape tablespoonfuls of the dough into balls and roll in the sugar mixture. Place the balls 1½in (4cm) apart on a cookie sheet and flatten slightly with the palm of your hand.
- Bake for 6–8 minutes. Immediately transfer to a wire rack to cool.

· SPONGE CAKE ·

8oz (250g) butter, softened
2 teaspoons vanilla extract
1 teaspoon finely grated
  lemon zest
2 cups superfine (caster)
  sugar
6 eggs
1½ cups all-purpose (plain)
  flour
1 cup self-rising (self-
  raising) flour
1 cup natural yogurt

Lemon frosting
1½ cups confectioners'
  (icing) sugar, sifted
1 tablespoon lemon juice
2 tablespoons butter,
  softened
2 tablespoons shredded
  coconut, toasted

Makes 1 cake

- Preheat oven to 320°F (160°C).
- Place butter, vanilla extract and lemon zest in a bowl and beat until light and fluffy. Gradually add superfine sugar, beating well after each addition until mixture is creamy. Add eggs one at a time, beating well after each addition.
- Sift together all-purpose and self-rising flour. Fold flour mixture and yogurt, alternately, into butter mixture. Spoon batter into a buttered and lined 9in (23cm) square cake tin and bake for 1 hour or until cake is cooked when tested with a skewer. Stand in tin for 10 minutes before turning onto a wire rack to cool completely.
- To make frosting, place confectioners' sugar, lemon juice and butter in a bowl and mix until smooth. Add a little more lemon juice if necessary. Spread frosting over cake and sprinkle with coconut.

POWDER PUFFS

2 eggs, separated
pinch of salt
⅓ cup superfine (caster)
  sugar
few drops of vanilla extract
½ cup self-rising (self-
  raising) flour, sifted with
  2 tablespoons cornstarch
  (cornflour)
whipped cream
confectioners' (icing) sugar,
  to dust

Makes about 6–8

○ Preheat oven to 375°F (190°C).
○ Beat the egg whites and salt together until stiff. Add the superfine sugar gradually and beat well between each addition until mixture is thick and glossy. Beat in the egg yolks and vanilla and fold in the sifted flour and cornstarch.
○ Spoon into buttered round-based patty cake tins and bake in the center of the oven for 10–15 minutes. Allow to cool. Split in half, sandwich together with cream and dust with confectioners' sugar.

○ NOTE Powder puffs may be spooned or piped onto baking paper on baking trays and cooked in the upper half of the oven for 7–10 minutes. Allow to cool. To remove from paper, slightly wet the back of the paper and peel off. Sandwich together as above.

COCONUT MACAROONS

1⅓ cups dessicated coconut
⅓ cup sugar
2 tablespoons all-purpose (plain) flour
⅛ teaspoon salt
2 egg whites, whisked
½ teaspoon almond extract

Makes 20

- Preheat oven to 320°F (160°C). Lightly butter a baking sheet.
- Combine coconut, sugar, flour and salt in a bowl. Stir in egg whites and almond extract. Mix well.
- Drop teaspoonfuls onto the baking sheet. Bake for 15 minutes or until edges are brown. Remove from sheets at once.

RICH FRUIT CAKE

2lb (1kg) dried mixed fruit
1 cup dried dates, chopped
4oz (125g) butter
¾ cup brown sugar
1 teaspoon ground
    cinnamon
½ cup brandy
2 eggs, lightly beaten
1 cup all-purpose (plain)
    flour
½ cup self-rising (self-
    raising) flour

Makes 1 cake

- Preheat oven to 320°F (160°C).
- Place mixed fruit, dates, butter, sugar, cinnamon and ½ cup of water in a large saucepan and cook over a medium heat, stirring until butter melts. Bring to the boil, reduce heat and simmer uncovered for 3 minutes.
- Remove pan from heat and cool to room temperature.
- Stir brandy and eggs into fruit mixture. Sift together flour and self-rising flour, add to fruit mixture and mix well to combine. Spoon batter into a buttered and lined 9in (23cm) round tin and bake for 1¼–1½ hours or until cooked when tested with a skewer.
- Allow to stand in tins for 10 minutes before turning out to cool completely.

MELTING MOMENTS

7oz (200g) butter, at room temperature
¾ cup confectioners' (icing) sugar
1 cup all-purpose (plain) flour
1 cup cornstarch (cornflour)
½ teaspoon baking powder
½ cup raspberry jelly (jam)

Makes 16

- Preheat oven to 360°F (180°C). Lightly butter an oven tray.
- Cream butter and confectioners' sugar until light and fluffy. Sift flour, cornstarch and baking powder together. Add to butter mixture and mix well.
- Roll dough into balls the size of large marbles and place on the oven tray. Flatten slightly with a floured fork. Bake for 20 minutes or until cooked.
- Allow to cool completely, then sandwich two halves together with raspberry jelly. Repeat with remaining.

PEAR UPSIDE-DOWN PUDDING

¼ cup Demerara (raw)
  sugar
2 x 15oz (440g) canned
  pear halves, drained, with
  1 cup syrup reserved
8oz (250g) butter, softened
2 cups self-rising
  (self-raising) flour
1 cup superfine (caster)
  sugar
4 eggs
1 cup chopped walnuts
¼ cup maple syrup

Serves 8

- Preheat oven to 360°F (180°C).
- Sprinkle base of a deep buttered and lined 9in (23cm) round cake tin with raw sugar. Cut pear halves in half to form quarters and arrange cut-side up, over base.
- Place butter, flour, sugar and eggs in a food processor and process until smooth. Stir in walnuts. Carefully spoon batter over fruit in tin and bake for 1–1¼ hours, or until cooked when tested with a skewer.
- Place maple syrup and reserved pear juice in a saucepan over a medium heat and cook until syrup is reduced by half.
- Turn pudding onto a serving plate and pour over syrup. Serve with cream or ice cream.

LEMON SHORT STARS

¾ cup all-purpose (plain) flour

¾ cup rice flour

½ cup superfine (caster) sugar

4oz (125g) butter

1 egg yolk

2 tablespoons half and half (single) cream

1 cup confectioners' (icing) sugar

⅓ cup lemon juice

zest of 1 lemon

Makes 35

- Preheat oven to 375°F (190°C). Line 2 oven trays with baking paper.
- Mix flours and superfine sugar, then rub in the butter until the mixture resembles breadcrumbs. Beat the egg yolk, add to the flour mixture with the cream and mix to make a very stiff paste.
- Roll out to an even thickness and cut out cookies with a star-shaped cutter. Place on a baking tray and bake for about 15 minutes, until a pale golden brown.
- Meanwhile combine the confectioners' sugar, lemon juice and zest to make a topping.
- Remove from the oven and cool on a wire rack. Decorate with the lemon topping.

CITRUS DELICIOUS PUDDING

1 cup superfine (caster) sugar

4oz (125g) butter, softened

½ cup self-rising (self-raising) flour

1 tablespoon finely grated lemon zest

1 tablespoon finely grated orange zest

2 tablespoons lemon juice

2 tablespoons orange juice

2 eggs, separated

1 cup milk

Serves 6

- Preheat oven to 360°F (180°C).
- Place sugar and butter in a bowl and beat until light and fluffy. Stir in flour, lemon and orange zests, and lemon and orange juices.
- Place egg yolks and milk in a bowl and whisk to combine. Stir into citrus mixture.
- Place egg whites in a bowl and beat until stiff peaks form, then fold into batter. Spoon batter into a buttered 4-cup capacity ovenproof dish. Place dish in a baking pan with enough boiling water to come halfway up the sides of dish. Bake for 45 minutes or until cooked.

PRESERVES
AND
CONDIMENTS

...

PRESERVES AND CONDIMENTS

৹৹৹

In the not-too-distant past, especially during war-time or periods of Depression, 'waste not, want not' was a constant mantra. Turning excess fruit and vegetables into preserves is the perfect way to make sure good food doesn't go to waste, and to keep your pantry fully stocked. Whether spread over warm, buttered toast for breakfast, or used as a condiment at lunch or dinnertime, preserves are incredibly versatile, and these recipes will ensure you always have a good range at the ready.

৹ INGREDIENTS ৹

Fruit should be just ripe or slightly under-ripe. Riper fruit and vegetables will be suitable for chutneys and ketchups. Ensure to rinse, drain and dry fresh produce before use. Discard over-ripe berries and cut out bruises. You can use frozen fruit if you prefer – just remember to allow a bit more cooking time.

When it comes to jellies or jams, it's best not to worry about your waistline. Sugar combines with fruit and vegetables to develop the best taste, and also acts as an essential preservative, so don't be tempted to reduce the amount in the recipe. White sugar will usually serve, though brown sugar can be lovely in marmalade.

Note: In these recipes, sugar measurements are given in ounces and grams rather than cups, for the sake of accuracy.

In chutneys, you may use spices that are already ground, or infuse preserves with whole spices tied in muslin or in a spice ball. Alternatively, you can toast whole spices in a pan before grinding with a pestle and mortar.

Vinegar, particularly red or white wine varieties, will often be suitable for savory recipes, and its acidity helps in the preservation process. Clear malt vinegar will maintain the particular hues of the ingredients, while cider vinegar has a fruitier taste.

❧ EQUIPMENT ❧

Most preserves can be made with some very basic equipment – a saucepan, a wooden spoon and some jars – but a few other tools that can help are a preserving pan, which allows liquid to reduce quickly; a thermometer that clips to the side of the pan to ensure you don't overboil; a funnel to help you fill up your jars; and a mouli, a special kind of grater for making purée. Don't worry if you don't want to invest in these tools of the jammery, as you can certainly get along without them.

❧ BOTTLING ❧

Before you decant a preserve into containers, you need to make sure it is set. Take the pan off the heat while you are testing.

Some methods for checking if a jelly is set include: placing a small amount on a chilled plate and then freezing for one minute – if it wrinkles when you touch it with a finger, it's not ready; using a thermometer to check for the setting point of 220°F (105°C); or letting some preserve cool on a wooden spoon for a few seconds, then dropping it off the spoon and checking for 'flakes' that hang on the edge, which indicate the setting point has been reached.

Jars and bottles must be sterilized before you fill them and should not have any chips or cracks. One good method for cleaning jars is to wash them in hot soapy water, rinse and dry them, then place them on a baking tray in a cold oven. Heat the oven to 300°F (150°C) and 'bake' them for 15–20 minutes. Metal jam-jar lids can be sterilized in the same way. If you have the luxury of a dishwasher, make use of it for this purpose, running your jars and lids on the hottest cycle. Ideally, you should fill the jars when they are still hot.

Ladle the hot preserve into the jars, filling almost to the top. With thicker chutneys, you may need to push them down in the jar with a teaspoon, to remove air pockets. Then place a disc of waxed paper on top and screw the lid on tightly. Leave the jars to cool, then label them, using classic calligraphy and a proper ink pen!

You can keep most preserves for at least a year, stored in a cool, dry place. Once opened, they should be refrigerated and eaten within a few weeks.

APRICOT PRESERVE

10½oz (200g) dried
   apricots
3 cups water
2 tablespoons lemon juice
1lb 6oz (625g) granulated
   sugar

**Makes 4lb 6oz
   (2kg)**

- Place the apricots in a strainer and rinse under running water. Place in a bowl, add the water and allow to soak for several hours or overnight.
- Place the apricots and soaking water in a saucepan. Bring to the boil, turn down the heat to moderate, cover and cook for 20 minutes, until the apricots are very soft. Add the lemon juice and sugar; stir until all the sugar is dissolved.
- Reduce the heat and simmer, uncovered, until the setting point is reached (about 30 minutes). Stir occasionally to make sure the mixture is not catching on the bottom.
- As soon as the setting point is reached, remove from the heat. Allow to cool enough to place in warm, sterilized jars. Label and seal.

Apple & Ginger Jam
1912

Ginger
19/2

APPLE AND GINGER PRESERVE

3lb 5oz (1.5kg) cooking
  apples
2 cups water
juice and rind of 2 lemons
½ teaspoon ground ginger
½ teaspoon ground
  cinnamon
3lb 5oz (1.5kg) granulated
  sugar
4 tablespoons grated fresh
  ginger

**Makes 7lb 12oz
  (3.5kg)**

- Peel, core and dice the apples. The pectin in the apple peel and cores is needed, so tie them up in a muslin bag.
- Put the diced apple, water, lemon juice and rind, ground ginger and cinnamon, and the muslin bag in a saucepan. Cook until the apple is tender. Add the sugar and grated ginger, and cook slowly until the sugar has dissolved. Squeeze the pectin out of the muslin bag into the jam, then turn up the heat and boil very fast until the setting point is reached.
- Remove the saucepan from the heat and let the jam stand for 10 minutes, before spooning it into sterilized jars. Label and seal when cool.

FIG PRESERVE

2lb 3oz (1kg) dried figs,
   roughly chopped
8 cups water
rind, pips and juice of
   2 lemons
1 teaspoon fennel seeds
3 tablespoons pine nuts
2oz (60g) flaked almonds
1lb 10oz (725g) granulated
   sugar

**Makes 7lb 12oz
   (3.5kg)**

Soak the dried figs in 1 litre (2 pints) of water for several hours.

Put the lemon rind and pips into a muslin bag. Place the figs, remaining water, lemon juice and bag of rind and pips in a saucepan and bring to the boil. Simmer until the figs are tender, stirring constantly.

Add the fennel seeds, pine nuts, flaked almonds and sugar, then stir until the sugar dissolves. Squeeze the juice out of the muslin bag into the mixture and discard the bag. Boil, stirring constantly, until the setting point is reached.

Ladle the preserve into warm sterilized jars. Label and seal.

NOTE This dried fig preserve is very easy to make. It tastes delicious with ice cream, but don't use too much, because it is very rich.

RHUBARB AND ORANGE PRESERVE

2lb 3oz (1kg) rhubarb
1lb 10oz (725g)
  granulated sugar
300g raisins
juice and rind of 2 oranges
juice and rind of 1 lemon

**Makes 3lb 13oz
  (1.75kg)**

- Wash the rhubarb and cut it into 8in (20cm) lengths. Put it into a large saucepan and sprinkle the sugar over. Add the raisins, and the juice and grated rind of the oranges and lemon. Mix with a wooden spoon. Cover and allow to stand for 1 hour.
- Bring to the boil and cook slowly, stirring frequently, for about 30 minutes.
- Allow the preserve to cool slightly in the saucepan. Put into clean warm sterilized jars and cover at once. Do not forget to label the jars.

STRAWBERRY PRESERVE

4lb 6oz (2kg)
  granulated sugar
4lb 6oz (2kg)
  strawberries, hulled
juice and rind of 2 lemons

**Makes 8lb 13oz
  (4kg)**

- Warm the sugar in a slow oven. Put the strawberries and lemon in a saucepan and heat gently, stirring as the juice begins to flow out of the fruit. When the juice is coming to the boil, add the warmed sugar.
- After it has dissolved, bring the preserve to a rapid boil until it thickens and reaches the setting point (about 15–20 minutes).
- Remove from the heat and let stand for 15 minutes. Ladle into sterilized jars, label and seal.

- NOTE A perennial favourite, strawberry jelly or jam tastes delicious with warm fresh croissants and tea.

ORANGE MARMALADE

2lb 3oz (1kg) oranges
juice of 1 lemon
8 cups water
4lb 6oz (2kg)
  granulated sugar

**Makes 10lb 7½oz
  (4.75kg)**

- Cut the oranges in half and squeeze out the juice. Strain the juice into a saucepan. Cut the peel finely, and put the pips into a muslin bag. Combine the juice and rind of the oranges with the lemon juice, the bag of pips and the water in the saucepan. Bring slowly to the boil and simmer for up to 2 hours or until the rind is tender.
- Add the sugar and stir until it has dissolved. Take out the muslin bag and squeeze the pectin back into the marmalade. Bring to the boil and boil rapidly for about 10 minutes or until the setting point is reached.
- Remove from the heat, let the marmalade rest for 30 minutes, stir the fruit gently, and spoon into sterilized jars. Label and seal when cold.

APPLE CHUTNEY

3lb 5oz (1.5kg) cooking
  apples, peeled and finely
  chopped
17½oz (500g) onions,
  finely chopped
9oz (250g) granulated
  sugar
½ cup water
2 tablespoons chopped
  fresh ginger
1 teaspoon ground
  cinnamon
3 red chillies
½ tablespoon salt
1½ cups vinegar

**Makes 6lb 10oz
  (3kg)**

Combine all the ingredients and bring to the boil.
Simmer until the mixture thickens, and then ladle into
sterilized jars. Seal straight away, label and store for
3 months before opening.

NOTE This is lovely with roast pork or ham, served
hot or cold. It's excellent in a sandwich too, with any
meat or with cheese.

TOMATO CHUTNEY

4lb 6oz (2kg) tomatoes,
  peeled and roughly
  chopped
20 cloves garlic, roughly
  chopped
2 tablespoons chopped fresh
  ginger
3oz (90g) raisins
13oz (370g) granulated
  sugar
1 tablespoon salt
2 chillies
rind and juice of 1 lemon
½ teaspoon cumin seeds
½ teaspoon fennel seeds
½ teaspoon fenugreek
1½ cups white wine vinegar

**Makes 5lb 8oz
  (2.5kg)**

Combine all the ingredients in a saucepan, bring
to the boil, and simmer for 1½–2 hours, stirring
frequently, or until the chutney is thick. The cooking
time depends on how firm the tomatoes are; if they
are watery, it will take longer to cook.

Spoon into sterilized jars, seal, and store in a dark,
dry cupboard.

NOTE Tomato chutney jars can be dressed up and
put under the Christmas tree. By making chutneys
and jams through the year, you can give yourself an
easier and more economical Christmas.

PICKLED ONIONS

3lb 5oz (1.5kg)
  pickling onions
9oz (250g) salt
approximately 8 cups water
13oz (375g) granulated
  white sugar
12 whole cloves
2 tablespoons peppercorns
3 cups white vinegar

Serves 4

- Cut off the ends of the onions neatly, peel them, and place them in a glass bowl. Dissolve the salt in the water and pour over the onions. Be sure they are completely covered. Place a piece of plastic wrap on top of the bowl and cover with a small plate or saucer. This will keep the onions submerged. Leave to stand for 18–24 hours.
- Place the sugar, cloves, peppercorns and vinegar in a stainless steel or enamel saucepan and bring slowly to the boil. Remove from the heat, cover, and leave to stand for 12–18 hours.
- Drain the onions and rinse well. Pack into jars and cover with the strained spiced vinegar. You can leave a few peppercorns and cloves in the vinegar, but too many will produce a very murky appearance. Cover and leave for 1 month.

BEET AND HORSERADISH PICKLE

2lb 3oz (1kg) beets
   (beetroot)
2oz (60g) horseradish relish
½ cup sugar
2½ cups wine vinegar
1 teaspoon salt
½ teaspoon fennel seeds
6 juniper berries

**Makes 2lb 3oz
   (1 kg)**

- In a large pot of water, boil the beets for 30 minutes. Cool, then peel. If they are large, cut into wedges, if small leave whole. Mix together beets and horseradish relish and pack into hot, sterilized jars.
- Meanwhile place sugar, vinegar, salt, fennel seeds and juniper berries into a saucepan and simmer for 15 minutes. Pour hot mixture over beetroot and seal. Store in refrigerator for 8–10 days to allow taste to develop before eating.

TEA PARTY
TREATS

...

TEA PARTY TREATS

°°°

Whether it's friends dropping by for coffee and cake, or an elegant luncheon celebration, the catering is an essential – if not *the* essential – element in a successful tea party.

◦ BEVERAGES ◦

For comforting taste and aroma, nothing beats tea. Keep a selection of favourites to hand, such as English Breakfast, Earl Grey and Ceylon, as well as a range of herbals teas that will satisfy anyone's needs. Some have remedial benefits – peppermint, for example, will settle an upset stomach. Where possible, try and use fresh tealeaves. Offer guests sugar, milk, honey and lemon, according to their preference.

Beautiful vintage tea sets can be discovered in secondhand junk shops and yard sales the world over, complete with matching cups, milk jugs and teapot. Floral designs are typical. If a complete set cannot be found, mismatched but complimentary pieces can look wonderfully retro and interesting.

These days, coffee should always be an option. Keep high-quality coffee grind in the freezer to retain its freshness. Most of us don't have our own espresso machine, but a traditional French press or an Italian Moka pot, which can be heated on the stove, will do perfectly. Make sure to check how strong your guests like their coffee.

Alcoholic beverages may be appropriate, depending on the occasion. Champagne or sparkling wine is a special touch for any celebration, served with a classic strawberry, while traditional cocktails – Tom Collins, Gin Slings, Sidecars and Manhattans, for example – will go down well for late afternoon or pre-dinner drinks.

◇ CAKES AND PASTRIES ◇

For a morning or afternoon gathering, nothing is lovelier than a freshly baked cake, presented on a beautiful stand or platter. Again, these are available second-hand for next to nothing, or might be handed down from your mother or grandmother. Don't reserve these treasures for special occasions. Beautiful tableware is supposed to be used.

While offering up a whole cake is easiest for a small, informal gathering (consult the index for cake recipes), a more elaborate soirée might require more sophisticated fare. A range of sweets, to be handed around the room like finger food, will work well and recipes are featured in this chapter.

◇ HORS D'OEUVRES ◇

For that touch of class, finger food is easy to put together, especially when it can be served cold and prepared in advance. Smoked salmon canapés or stuffed cherry tomatoes are lovely arranged on a serving platter. Delicate whitebread sandwiches – cut into quarters or fingers, with the crusts removed – are delicious if kept simple, and will evoke memories of picnics and parties past.

◇ DÉCOR ◇

Fresh flowers are always the best decoration and don't need to be expensive. Choose whatever is blossoming in your garden, or just a sweet, cheap bunch of daisies.

If you're sitting down to cake and coffee, or sandwiches and snacks, lay the table with a patterned tablecloth or a fresh piece of linen. Also put out some cotton napkins, and whatever cutlery and crockery you need, but don't fuss too much about these details – a tea party of any kind is first and foremost about catching up and relaxing with friends and family.

TRADITIONAL SCONES

2 cups self-rising
  (self-raising) flour
1 teaspoon baking powder
2 teaspoons sugar
1½oz (45g) butter
1 egg
½ cup milk

Makes 12

- Preheat the oven to 430°F (220°C). Sift together flour and baking powder into a large bowl. Stir in sugar, then rub in butter, using fingertips, until mixture resembles coarse breadcrumbs.
- Whisk together egg and milk. Make a well in the center of the flour mixture, pour in egg mixture and mix to form a soft dough. Turn onto a lightly floured surface and knead lightly.
- Press dough out to a ¾in (2cm) thickness, using palm of hand. Cut out scones using a floured 2in (5cm) cutter. Avoid twisting the cutter, or the scones will rise unevenly.
- Arrange scones close together on a greased and lightly floured baking tray or in a shallow 8in (20cm) round cake tin. Brush with a little milk and bake for 12–15 minutes or until golden. Eat immediately, with strawberry preserve (page 183) and whipped cream.

APPLE SCONES

2 cups all-purpose (plain)
  flour
¼ cup granulated sugar
2 teaspoons baking powder
½ teaspoon baking soda
  (bicarbonate of soda)
½ teaspoon salt
1½oz (45g) butter, chilled
1 large apple, peeled and
  grated
½ cup milk

Makes 12

- Preheat oven to 430°F (220°C). Combine flour, sugar, baking powder, baking soda and salt in a large bowl. Cut in butter until crumbly.
- Add apple and milk. Stir to form soft dough. Turn out onto lightly floured surface. Knead gently until combined. Pat into two 6in (15cm) circles. Place on buttered baking sheet. Brush tops with milk. Sprinkle with sugar, then with cinnamon. Score each top into six pie-shaped wedges.
- Bake for 15 minutes until browned and risen. Serve warm with butter.

CHEESE SCONES

1⅓ cup self-rising
  (self-raising) flour
¼ teaspoon Cayenne pepper
1 teaspoon salt
2oz (60g) butter
1 tablespoon finely chopped
  onion
2oz (60g) Cheddar cheese,
  grated
1 egg
¼ cup parsley, finely
  chopped
2 cups milk, plus ¼ cup
  extra
1 egg, beaten

Makes 12-16

- Preheat oven to 450°F (230°C).
- Sift flour, pepper and salt then, using fingertips, rub butter into the flour mixture. Add onion, cheese, egg and parsley. Make a well in the center and add the 2 cups of milk all at once, stirring quickly and lightly to a soft dough.
- Turn onto a lightly floured board and knead just enough to make a smooth surface. Pat into ½–¾in (12–18mm) thickness and, using a small cutter, cut into rounds.
- Place on a floured baking tray. Brush tops with combined beaten egg and milk and then bake for about 10 minutes.

· DATE SCONES ·

1⅓ cup self-rising
  (self-raising) flour
1 teaspoon salt
2 teaspoons ground
  cinnamon
2oz (60g) butter
4oz (125g) chopped dates
2 tablespoons sugar
2 cups milk, plus ¼ cup
  extra
1 egg

Makes 12–16

- Preheat oven to 450°F (230°C).
- Sift flour, salt and cinnamon then, using fingertips, rub butter into the flour mixture. Add dates and sugar. Make a well in the center and add the 2 cups of milk all at once, stirring quickly and lightly to a soft dough.
- Turn onto a lightly floured board and knead just enough to make a smooth surface. Pat into ½–¾in (12–18mm) thickness and, using a small scone cutter, cut into rounds.
- Place on a floured baking tray. Brush tops with combined beaten egg and milk and then bake for about 10 minutes.

HOT CROSS BUNS

3 x ¼oz (7g) sachets yeast
1 cup lukewarm milk
pinch of salt
2 tablespoons light brown
  sugar
1 teaspoon ground
  cinnamon
½ teaspoon ground nutmeg
¼ teaspoon ground allspice
2 eggs
4 cups all-purpose (plain)
  flour
2 tablespoons vegetable oil
2 tablespoons mixed fruit
  peel
2 tablespoons raisins

Cross
½ cup all-purpose (plain)
  flour

Glaze
½ teaspoon gelatin
2 tablespoons confectioners'
  (icing) sugar
2 tablespoons warm no-fat
  (skim) milk

Makes 18

- Place yeast in a large bowl. Pour in milk. Stand in warm place for 10 minutes or until frothy. Stir in salt, sugar and spices. Beat in eggs, one at a time. Stir in half the flour to make a soft dough. Beat in oil. Continue beating for 1 minute. Knead in remaining flour. Place dough in a lightly oiled bowl. Turn to coat with oil. Cover with cling wrap. Stand in a warm place for 1 hour or until doubled in size.
- Knead dough, working in mixed fruit peel and raisins on a lightly floured surface. Roll into a log. Cut into 18 even-sized pieces. Shape pieces into buns.
- Place buns, 1in (2.5cm) apart, on buttered baking trays. Cover. Stand in a warm place for 20 minutes.
- For the cross, place flour and ⅓ cup water in a bowl. Beat until smooth. Spoon cross mixture into a piping bag fitted with a small plain nozzle. Mark a cross on top each bun.
- Preheat oven to 400°F (200°C). Bake buns for 15 minutes or until golden.
- For the glaze, place all ingredients in a bowl. Mix until smooth. Brush warm buns with glaze.

BUTTERSCOTCH BUNS

2oz (60g) butter, softened, plus 1½oz (45g) chilled
¾ cup brown sugar, packed
2 cups all-purpose (plain) flour
2 tablespoons granulated sugar
4 teaspoons baking powder
1 teaspoon salt
¾ cup milk
⅓ cup chopped nuts

Makes 12

- Preheat oven to 430°F (220°C). Cream softened butter and brown sugar together in a small bowl. Set aside.
- In a large bowl, combine flour, sugar, baking powder and salt. Cut in chilled butter until mixture is crumbly. Make a well in the center.
- Pour milk into the well. Stir to make a soft dough. Knead 8–10 times. Pat or roll out on a lightly floured surface into a 9–10in (23–25cm) square. Spread with brown sugar mixture. Sprinkle with nuts.
- Roll up as for a jelly roll, and pinch edge to seal. Cut into 12 slices. Place on buttered 8in (20cm) pan. Bake 15–20 minutes. Invert over tray while hot.

RASPBERRY CAKES

1 cup whole wheat
  self-rising (wholemeal
  self-raising) flour
1 cup white self-rising
  (self-raising) flour
½ cup bran
½ teaspoon baking soda
  (bicarbonate of soda)
1 teaspoon ground ginger
¾ cup buttermilk
⅓ cup orange juice
  concentrate
2 eggs
⅔ cup fresh, or frozen and
  partly thawed, raspberries

Makes 10

- Preheat oven to 360°F (180°C). Sift dry ingredients into a bowl. Return any bran to the bowl.
- Beat together buttermilk, orange juice and eggs. Pour into dry ingredients, all at once. Add raspberries and mix until just combined – take care not to overmix. Spoon into buttered muffin pans.
- Bake for 20–25 minutes or until cooked when tested with a skewer.

PUMPKIN CAKES

1½ cups all-purpose (plain)
  flour
1 teaspoon baking powder
1 teaspoon baking soda
  (bicarbonate of soda)
½ teaspoon salt
½ teaspoon ground
  cinnamon
½ teaspoon ground nutmeg
½ teaspoon ground ginger
½ cup raisins
1 egg
¼ cup granulated sugar
⅓ cup olive oil
1 cup cooked pumpkin
½ cup milk

Makes 12

- Preheat oven to 400°F (200°C). Combine flour, baking powder, baking soda, salt, cinnamon, nutmeg, ginger and raisins in a large bowl. Stir thoroughly. Make a well in the center.
- In a small bowl, beat egg until frothy. Mix sugar, oil, pumpkin and milk and pour into well. Stir only to moisten. Batter will be lumpy.
- Fill buttered muffin cups three-quarters full. Bake for 15–20 minutes. Let stand 5 minutes. Remove from pan. Serve warm. Dust with confectioners' sugar.

RAISIN CAKES

1½ cups all-purpose (plain)
  flour, sifted
2 teaspoons baking powder
½ teaspoon salt
¼ cup Demerara (raw)
  sugar
1 cup seeded raisins
¾ cup milk
1 egg
1½oz (45g) butter, melted

Makes 12

- Preheat oven to 360°F (180°C). Butter 12 medium muffin tins.
- In a medium bowl, sift together flour, baking powder, salt and sugar. Mix in raisins.
- Place egg, milk and butter in a small bowl and whisk to combine. Pour milk mixture into dry ingredients and mix with a fork until ingredients are just combined, do not over-mix.
- Spoon mixture into 12 buttered muffin tins. Bake for 20–25 minutes or until cakes are cooked when tested with a skewer. Turn onto wire racks to cool.

CHOCOLATE RUM SLICES

1 cup self-rising
  (self-raising) flour, sifted
1 tablespoon cocoa powder,
  sifted
½ cup superfine (caster)
  sugar
2½oz (75g) desiccated
  coconut
2½oz (75g) raisins, chopped
4oz (125g) butter, melted
1 teaspoon rum
2 tablespoons grated
  semisweet (dark) chocolate
2 eggs, lightly beaten

Chocolate topping
1 cup confectioners' (icing)
  sugar
2 tablespoons cocoa powder
½oz (15g) butter, softened

Makes 25

- Preheat oven to 360°F (180°C). Place flour, cocoa powder, superfine sugar, coconut and raisins in a bowl and mix to combine. Stir in butter, rum, grated chocolate and eggs. Mix well.
- Press mixture into a buttered and lined 10in (25cm) square cake tin and bake for 20–25 minutes or until firm. Allow to cool in tin.
- To make topping, sift confectioners' sugar and cocoa powder together into a bowl. Add butter and 1 tablespoon boiling water, and beat to make topping of a spreadable consistency.
- Turn slice onto a wire rack or plate, spread with topping and sprinkle with extra coconut. Refrigerate until firm, then cut into squares.

CARAMEL SQUARES

Shortbread base
3½oz (100g) butter
3 tablespoons sugar
¾ cup cornstarch
   (cornflour), sifted
¾ cup all-purpose (plain)
   flour, sifted

Caramel filling
4oz (125g) butter
½ cup brown sugar
2 tablespoons honey
14oz (400g) sweetened
   condensed milk
1 teaspoon vanilla extract

Chocolate topping
7oz (200g) semisweet
   (dark) chocolate, melted

Makes 24

- Preheat oven to 360°F (180°C). To make base, place butter and sugar in a bowl and beat until light and fluffy. Mix in cornstarch and flour, turn onto a lightly floured surface and knead briefly, then press into a buttered and lined 8 x 12in (20 x 30cm) shallow cake tin and bake for 25 minutes or until firm.
- To make filling, place butter, brown sugar and honey in a saucepan and cook over a medium heat, stirring constantly until sugar melts and ingredients are combined. Bring to the boil and simmer for 7 minutes. Beat in condensed milk and vanilla extract, pour filling over base and bake for 20 minutes longer.
- Set aside to cool completely. Spread melted chocolate over filling, set aside until firm, then cut into squares.

CHOC-MINT BROWNIES

4oz (125g) butter
7oz (200g) dark chocolate,
  grated
2 eggs
¾ cup brown sugar
2 tablespoons cocoa powder
2 tablespoons oil
1 cup all-purpose (plain)
  flour

Topping
1 cup confectioners' (icing)
  sugar
½oz (15g) butter
3 drops peppermint extract

Makes 20

- Preheat oven to 320°F (160°C).
- Melt butter and chocolate in a medium saucepan, stir until combined, then cool slightly. Beat eggs and sugar until light and creamy. Beat in cocoa and oil, then beat in flour and cooled chocolate mixture.
- Pour mixture into a buttered and lined 9 x 9in (23 x 23cm) square tin. Bake for 40 minutes or until cooked when tested with a skewer. Turn onto wire rack to cool.
- To make the topping, sift confectioners' sugar into a heatproof bowl, add butter and peppermint extract, and stir over simmering water until smooth. Drizzle or pipe topping over top of brownies. Cut into squares and serve.

. PLUM .
PUDDING

margarine to grease the
   basin
2 tablespoons plum jelly
   (jam)
2oz (60g) butter
¼ cup sugar
1 egg
½ cup all-purpose (plain)
   flour
1 teaspoon gluten-free
   baking powder
1 tablespoon milk

Serves 3

- Place a saucepan that will fit a 5 x 2in (13 x 6cm) deep fluted pudding basin on to boil, with enough water to come halfway up the pudding basin. Make sure that you have a tight-fitting lid for the saucepan.
- Grease the pudding basin with margarine, and cut a piece of greaseproof paper large enough to fit the top of the basin. The paper should be larger than the basin so that it will not let any water in when the pudding is steaming.
- Place the plum jelly in the bottom of the greased pudding basin. Cream the butter, sugar and egg together until fluffy. Fold in the sifted flour and baking powder. Stir in the milk and pour into the pudding basin. Lower the pudding into the boiling water. Loosely lay the greaseproof paper on top of the pudding.
- Place the lid on the saucepan and keep the water boiling for about 40 minutes. When cooked, turn the pudding out onto a plate and serve with custard or ice cream.

RASPBERRY TART

1 sheet shortcrust pastry
1½ cups frozen raspberries
½ cup superfine (caster)
  sugar
juice of ½ lemon
confectioners' (icing) sugar
  and whipped cream to
  serve

Serves 6

- Preheat the oven to 400°F (200°C).
- Line a baking tray with baking paper, place a ring mold onto the tray. Cut a large round from the pastry and use it to line the base and sides of the mold, to form a tart case. Trim the excess pastry. Bake blind for 6–8 minutes or until the pastry is light golden.
- Place the raspberries and sugar in a bowl, add the lemon juice and microwave for 6–8 minutes on high (100%) or until thickened like a preserve.
- Remove the mold from the pastry case. Spoon the raspberry into the pastry case and allow to cool before serving. Dust with confectioner's sugar and serve with whipped cream.

APPLE TARTS

1–2 sheets shortcrust pastry
17½oz (500g) apples,
 peeled and cored
juice and zest of 1 lemon
¼ cup sugar
1oz (30g) butter
2 eggs, lightly beaten
⅓ cup blackberry jelly (jam)

Makes 8

- Preheat oven to 400°F (200°C). Line 8 patty tins with the pastry, prick with a fork and cook for about 10–15 minutes, until browned. Cook the apples with water for 15 minutes.
- When cooked, rub through a sieve, return to the saucepan and add lemon zest, juice, sugar, butter and eggs. Allow to cook over a low heat until the mixture thickens slightly.
- Place a teaspoon or two of the jam in the bottom of each pastry case and then fill the cases with the apple mixture and return to oven to set. Serve sprinkled with sifted confectioners' (icing) sugar.

EGG SANDWICHES

5 hard-boiled eggs, shelled
dash of Tabasco sauce
10 slices white bread
1oz (30g) butter, at room
    temperature
¼ bunch watercress

Mayonnaise
1 egg yolk
½ teaspoon salt
½ teaspoon wholegrain
    mustard
⅔ cup extra-light virgin
    olive oil
1 teaspoon sherry vinegar
freshly ground black pepper

Makes 20

- To make the mayonnaise, place egg yolk, salt and mustard in a bowl. Beat vigorously with a wooden spoon until thickened. Add a quarter of the oil, drop by drop, then stir in half the vinegar. Gradually add remaining oil in a thin stream, beating constantly. Stir in remaining vinegar and season to taste with black pepper. If too thin, add 1–2 tablespoons boiling hot water, beating well.
- Roughly chop hard-boiled eggs and stir into mayonnaise. Season to taste with Tabasco. Butter the bread, then spread egg mixture on half the slices, top with watercress and remaining bread slices. Press firmly, wrap and chill for 1 hour.
- Trim crusts and cut each sandwich into fingers.

CHICKEN AND WALNUT SANDWICHES

½ tablespoon cream cheese
  (softened)
½ tablespoon mayonnaise
1 tablespoon milk
a handful of walnuts, finely
  chopped
3½oz (100g) poached
  chicken breast, shredded
1 tablespoon flat-leaf
  parsley, chopped
salt and black pepper
4 slices soft whole wheat
  (wholemeal) fresh bread,
  lightly buttered

Makes 12

○ Mix the cream cheese and mayonnaise together. If a more liquid consistency is needed to coat the chicken, add a small quantity of milk.
○ Stir the walnuts into the mayonnaise mixture.
○ Add the shredded chicken and chopped parsley, and mix to combine. Season to taste.
○ Divide the mixture onto two slices of fresh bread and top with the other slices.
○ Trim crusts off sandwich and cut into three fingers, then cut each finger in half.

CRISPY STUFFED MUSHROOMS

2 cups fresh white
  breadcrumbs
2 tbsp finely chopped shaved
  ham
1 tbsp finely chopped cherry
  tomatoes
1 tbsp sliced chives
2 tbsp melted butter
Salt and freshly ground
  black pepper
2 eggs, lightly beaten
24 button mushrooms, stalks
  removed
Vegetable oil for frying

Makes 24

- Combine a third of a cup of breadcrumbs with the ham, tomatoes, chives, butter, salt and pepper in a bowl.
- Fill mushrooms evenly with stuffing.
- Place eggs and remaining breadcrumbs in two separate bowls. Dip mushrooms into the egg and then coat in breadcrumbs.
- Heat enough oil in a deep pan. Deep-fry mushrooms in batches for 1–2 minutes or until golden and crisp. Leave to cool a little and then serve.

CHICKEN LIVER SPREAD

1 onion, finely chopped
1 clove garlic, finely chopped
1 rasher bacon, finely
   chopped
4 oz (125g) butter
8 oz (250g) chicken livers,
   cleaned
½ tsp fresh thyme, chopped
Salt and freshly ground
   black pepper
¼ cup cream
1 tbsp brandy
1 packet water crackers

Serves 4

- Melt butter in a frypan. Add the onion, garlic and bacon, and cook until tender.
- Add chicken livers, thyme, salt and pepper. Cook for a further 5 minutes.
- Allow to cool slightly then place in a food processor and process until smooth.
- Add brandy and cream and process until well combined.
- Place into a large mould and surround with crackers.

ROAST BEEF WITH SWEET ONION

2 tbsp olive oil

2 medium onions, halved and thinly sliced

1½ tbsp balsamic vinegar

1 tbsp brown sugar

1½ tbsp thyme leaves

1 french bread stick or baguette, cut into ¾in (1½cm) slices

Olive oil spray

⅓ cup light cream cheese

14 large, thin slices of rare roast beef, cut in half

Makes about 28

- Preheat oven to 440°F (220°C).
- Heat oil in a saucepan over low heat. Cook onion for 10 minutes, or until soft, stirring from time to time. Add balsamic vinegar and brown sugar. Cover and cook for a further 15 minutes, or until caramelized, stirring from time to time. Transfer onions to a bowl and stir in thyme leaves.
- Meanwhile, place bread slices on a baking tray and spray with olive oil. Place in the oven and cook for 5–6 minutes or until just golden.
- Spread bread evenly with cream cheese, top with roast beef and caramelized onions.

RECIPE INDEX